CO-CREATING DEEPER CONNECTIONS IN YOUR REAL RELATIONSHIP

Belden Johnson
Marriage and Family Therapist

Also by Belden Johnson:

Real Relationship: Essential Tools to Help You Go the Distance
Fathers and Teachers: A Novel
Snake Blossoms: Fabulations

www.centerforinnervisions.com

Cover design by CreateSpace Project Team
Interior typesetting by Michelle Lovi at Odyssey Books

To my grandchildren

ACKNOWLEDGEMENTS

For their always prescient assistance in clarifying my thinking on most of these matters over the years I wish to thank Dr. Yashi Johnson and Dr. Stephen Khamsi.

For her talented hand in producing the artwork for Maslow's pyramid, my deepest thanks to my wonderful daughter-in-law, Sandra Reboucas Johnson.

The cover image of Picasso's "The Lovers" is courtesy of the National Gallery, Washington, D.C.

CONTENTS

FOREWORD

by
Dr. Stephen Khamsi

Welcome to the real world. Here's that map that you were looking for. The one that you need about relationships, which is probably the most important thing in your life. *Co-Creating Deeper Connections in Your Real Relationship* stands alone and also continues the story from Belden's previous book, *Real Relationship*. Both books offer a unique philosophy—as well as step-by-step instructions and a long list of personal and interpersonal exercises—for creating and reviving real consciousness and real love.

Perhaps you're already familiar with *Real Relationship* and its essential tools for going the distance. That's a great start and—in any event—you can now begin or continue the journey. *Co-Creating Deeper Connections in Your Real Relationship* introduces seven tools that are essential for strengthening and deepening your relationship. These seven tools add to those that were introduced in *Real Relationship*.

Ready to start? Couples need to orient themselves with a compass, a map, a GPS. While in relationship, we need to know who we are, where we've been, what we need, what we're trying to do, and where we're trying to go. Relationships can be fun and fulfilling, even scintillating and transcendental. But failed relationships can tragically break one's heart, crush one's spirit, or splinter an entire family.

You are hereby invited into the thoughts, the wisdom, and the musings of long-time marriage and family therapist par excellence Belden Crane Johnson. This is a book that delivers unprecedented personal sharing, and you'll enjoy the ride. Belden lives life well and herein shares time-tested ideas and strategies about intimacy, about boundaries, and about our passions and priorities. At first glance, it might seem simple: just engage in the seven suggestions that are listed in the first seven chapters—those that are clearly labeled in the Table of Contents.

What could possibly go wrong? Much of co-creating, after all, is based on simple principles and common sense. And yet we all know that most relationships bog down and sometimes even dissolve over time. Many couples need expert support and guidance along the way. Here you will find existential lessons about honesty and empathy, kindness and compassion, acceptance and loss, denial and defensiveness, passion and pain, trust and transparency, temptation and desire, self-care and self-protection, connection and coupleship, transgression and redemption.

Belden is an expert on sex and love, fidelity and infidelity. He is that unusual and accomplished individual who is both modest and bold—a mature thinker and a compassionate person, a scrupulous man with an open mind and a steady moral compass. He can be folksy and funny, literary and scholarly—but he's mostly a brave and brilliant writer, thinker and therapist with uncommon insights. His message? Real relationships require strong values, solid commitments, clear communication, and lots of hard work. Belden challenges, supports and guides the reader to be and become their best self by engaging in radical introspection and interpersonal risk-taking. Risk? Life requires that we take risks, and risks that are well-conceived and successful are inspirational and good. There are ways to turn ordinary fidelity, even infidelity, into high fidelity—and it's infinitely better to do so before the affair, rather than after.

There's quite a range here, from struggles and snuggles … to pillow talk and pillow-pounding … to drumming and dreaming and beyond. The universe is a positive place, and explorers are encouraged to expand their spiritual lives, to self-actualize, to break on through, to heal person and family and planet, to let go at times while never giving up or giving in.

In sum, *Co-Creating* does many things well. First of all, there are rich descriptions of specific couples—including their power struggles, their set-backs, and their triumphs—as they journey forth. *Co-Creating* also provides clear translations of big ideas and esoteric experiences into, well, something entirely comprehensible and livable. Plus it provides a new lexicon that allows readers to augment their own thinking and feeling and experiencing. It challenges readers to become more present and centered, more balanced and loving. To become a better person and partner who's capable of creating a solid foundation and who's capable of ascending, no matter the thunder or the wind or the rain. It's as elemental as earth, air, water and fire, and it's real.

Glen Ellen, California
July, 2014

INTRODUCTION

Those who restrain their desires have desires
weak enough to be restrained.
—Wm. Blake

Human beings face a troubling inner contradiction: We are psycho-socially primed for one lifelong mate and biologically oriented toward having several. When we first fall in love and are swept up in the cascade of chemicals that comprise the Love Cocktail, we are certain that we have found our soul mate and that we will love each other forever in complete fidelity. This state, however, is a temporary if blissful insanity, usually lasting no more than a couple of years and sometimes much less. As the Cocktail depletes, most of us find ourselves highly susceptible to a new attraction. While it is socially sanctioned for us to feel guilty and berate ourselves for being so fickle, in fact we are just behaving as Ma Nature has programmed us, in some very powerful ways.

Recent research informs us that somewhere between forty and seventy per cent of married people of both genders will admit to having had at least one outside sexual contact during their marriages. In other words, affairs are *normal*, in the sense that they are what most people do.[1] The traditional assumptions that (1) if we love someone we won't be

---

1   Research on marital infidelity is understandably problematic. Few people will readily divulge that they have had or are having a sexual contact outside of their marriage. The more anonymity, the more likely they are to cop to it. Thus the wide range in the statistics. The high end was reported in S. Hite, *The Hite Report* (1987).

attracted to anyone else and that (2) willpower will overcome any temptation even if we are, have been shown by careful research to be wishful thinking.[2]

For those of us who would like to grow a vivid long-term relationship that defies these odds, we will have to face the facts squarely and then quite mindfully construct some sturdy seawalls that can withstand the forceful tides and tsunamis of our genetic programming. Having spent most of a lifetime wrestling with this conundrum, both as a fallible human being and as a therapist, I have discovered some stout stones and mortar for building such a seawall. In *Real Relationship: Essential Tools to Help You Go the Distance* (2011), I offered tools for keeping feelings alive, for dealing with the ghosts of the past, for treating one another with kindness, and for developing clear communications, including being able to manage conflict constructively. These fundamental tools will go a long way toward protecting your relationship.

Why, some people will ask, do we need to spend so much time and effort working at strengthening our relationships? If we love each other, won't that be enough?

In a word, No. Love is not enough.

I call this the Happily-Ever-After Myth. It's just that: a myth. Long-term relationships don't happen like apples in Eden. They're a lot of hard, hard work.

I am often struck by the irony that most people spend more time, effort, and money on the maintenance of their automobiles than they do on the maintenance of their relationships. One man I know used to wash and wipe down his

---

2   See, e.g., Baumeister, R. & Tierney, J., *Willpower* (2011) and DeSteno, D., and Valdesolo, P., *Out of Character: Surprising Truths About the Liar, Cheat, Sinner (and Saint) Lurking in All of Us* (2011).

car at the end of each working day. Meanwhile, his wife, who thought he cared more about his car than her, began spending time "working out" with another man. Fortunately, her husband began putting his car in the garage with a few dust motes on it and spending that half hour a day with his wife. It saved their marriage.

We need to spend *more* time and effort maintaining our relationships than we do on maintaining our vehicles, our households, and our bodies *combined*.

Unless, I should add in fairness, you are happy with short-term relating. If you're content with a series of one- or two-year relationships, the Love Cocktail is enough. Nothing wrong with choosing that path, so long as you and your partners are clear that's what you're doing. In that case, you don't need this book. Pass it on to a friend who wants to go the distance.

This book is for people who value both continuity and aliveness in their relationships. Who want to stay together passionately for a long, long time. Who are willing to invest the time and effort to deepen their connections. Who want to give themselves the best chances for not being snagged in an affair.

I want to make it clear from the onset that, given our human nature, blindly believing that neither partner will ever have an affair is a pie-in-the-sky expectation for most of us. What we can do is to put in place strong structures that will (a) minimize the likelihood of an affair and (b) lay the groundwork for a positive recovery from a misstep. With experienced affair-recovery counseling, nine out of ten couples can rebuild their relationship.[3]

---

3   So says Rick Reynolds, LCSW, founder of Affair Recovery in Austin, Texas, who's been reconnecting couples for over 20 years.

The basic purpose of this book is to help you further strengthen your relationship by becoming mindful of and practicing some powerful ways of deepening your connection. Doing so will minimize the likelihood of an affair happening. If you are already dealing with an affair, however, I encourage you to take the coupleship to a good affair-recovery therapist immediately.

In the book you are holding I am going to give you seven additional tools for building a relationship that can weather the stormy blasts and the changing tides of our lives. These tools are: Meeting each other's primary needs, being totally honest, having joyful sex together, spending quality time together (and apart), playing and laughing together, exploring Inner Space together, and developing or deepening your spiritual connection.

Please understand that these seven tools do not stand alone but are add-ons for the important ones that I gave you in *Real Relationship: Essential Tools to Help You Go the Distance*. If you haven't done so already, please read that book first.

My interest—perhaps I should say obsession—with relationships and how to protect them originated in my own seeming predilection for straying. I rationalized that I had a high sex drive and might be a love addict. Because I wished to live honestly, I chose to be in an open relationship[4] for some seven years, thereby solving the paradox of wanting a deep, long-term relationship while being free to follow my heart, and loins, wherever they led. Although I have the

---

4   See O'Neill & O'Neill, *Open Marriage* (1984) and Easton & Hardy, *The Ethical Slut* (2009).

highest respect for those who choose to live such an open lifestyle in what is now called polyamory, I finally decided to choose monogamy. I knew that manifesting that choice would not be easy for me. I knew myself painfully well and I had read the research on our biological programming. So I set out to collect the most practical means available that would help me remain monogamous. They have worked for me for over a quarter century. I say that with some pride but also with the great humility of one who knows how vulnerable any of us is to a powerful surge of mind-made chemicals. As the Yiddish proverb puts it, "Man plans, God laughs."

I cannot promise you that if you read this book neither you nor your partner will ever have an affair. What I can promise is that you are less likely to lose your relationship. I can also promise you that, if you follow my suggestions in this book and in *Real Relationship*, you will grow into a better person, one who is more understanding, more compassionate, kinder, and more accepting. These are four of the more important components of true love. You will become more loving.

Please remember, as I told you in *Real Relationship*, that relationships are hard work. Just being around the same person day after day isn't easy, as most of us who have grown up in families know from experience. The French existentialist philosopher Jean Paul Sartre asserted in this play *No Exit* that "Hell is other people." He was a real grouch. But it's certainly true that anyone can be annoying when we are forced to live cheek to jowl. The human brain has a "negativity bias," which means that when it doesn't know something it will assume the worst. Lacking hard information, the brain will make up a dark story to fill the vacuum of ignorance. Sadly, people mostly don't know what they are doing or why. We perceive threat everywhere and react to those perceptions with lightning speed. The fight-flight-freeze response of the reptilian part of the brain is triggered far more quickly than the rational part of the brain can compensate. In this state we will assume the worst about our partners. Then we will build a case for why he or she is a terrible person and why this new person is so much nicer. If we wish to maintain a long-term relationship, we must learn how to outsmart our own brains. This book presents you with seven powerful means to do so.

CHAPTER 1:
MEET EACH OTHER'S NEEDS
(as often as you can)

Reason not the need.
—Wm. Shakespeare's King Lear

Ken and Kathy had been clients of mine three years ago when they were first deciding whether to get married and raise a family. Now they had a two-year old daughter and Ken wanted to come back in to address his growing frustration with what he called their "lack of connection."

"Having a child together has been awesome," he said. "I never imagined I could feel so much tender love. But Kathy and my's relationship is getting neglected. We're putting all our energy into being parents and almost nothing into our relationship. We've had very little sex in the last two years…"

"Well," Kathy interjected, "the doctor told us no more intercourse during the last trimester, and then, what with the episiotomy and a twelve hour labor I was in no shape—"

"I understood all that," Ken countered, "but that was two years ago. It seems like you're just not interested in sex anymore…"

"Well, I'm exhausted at the end of the day, after taking care of Tania and the house…."

I sighed. When they'd come in three years before, they got quite good at being able to listen to one another and to reflect back what each other was saying. Yet now they had regressed to batting the conversational ball back and forth across some invisible net and jumping in before the other had finished speaking, as if trying to outpoint the other.

Hearing my sigh, they both turned to me in surprise.

"I wonder," I said, "if you could slow down and use your Magic Mirrors to reflect what you're hearing. I know you can do that. Kathy, would you be willing just to hear Ken for a bit?"

Kathy nodded and turned to face Ken. He took a deep breath.

"Sweetheart, I love you," he said. "I want us to be close again."

Kathy burst into tears. Ken gathered her into his arms and wept with her.

Sometimes, that's all that it takes. Once they'd broken through the denial and defensiveness, Ken and Kathy were able to work out a program for how to re-prioritize their relationship and their sex life. They had two follow-up sessions to make sure they were on track and to fine-tune the adjustments they needed to make, but the breakthrough came when Ken was able to speak directly from his heart (which Kathy needed him to do) and Kathy was willing to truly hear what Ken needed (which Ken really needed Kathy to do).

However, I should point out what might be invisible. They both cared enough about the relationship to make the appointment with me, to speak honestly in it, and to be open to their feelings and to hearing one another. They had already learned some skills which they only needed to refresh. And they were willing to face and overcome discomfort. They each had a need to repair their relationship.

An Oversimplification

Let's begin with an oversimplification which, like all generalizations, is often false:

> *When our needs are not met within our relationship, we are quite vulnerable to the lure of an affair. When our needs are met within our relationship, we are likely to value that relationship above all others and to be vigilant in protecting it.*

Let's take a closer look at what exactly needs are.

I am using the word "need" less than precisely. "Wish" might be a better choice. The literal definition of "need" is something without which you will perish: For example, we all need air, water, and food to survive. The great American psychologist Abe Maslow[5] constructed what he called the "Hierarchy of Needs" in a five-level pyramid beginning with those physiological needs as well as the needs for sex, shelter, and warmth. At the second level are the safety needs, such as security of our bodies and resources. At the third level are the need to love and belong—in friendships, family, and intimacy with a partner. At the fourth level come our need for self-esteem, recognized achievement, and respect. At the top level is what Maslow called the need for self-actualization: the need to become who we truly are—an ethical, creative, spontaneous, loving human being:

After much study of healthy people, Maslow believed that every human being had all five levels of need. These are

---

5   *Motivation and Personality* (1954).

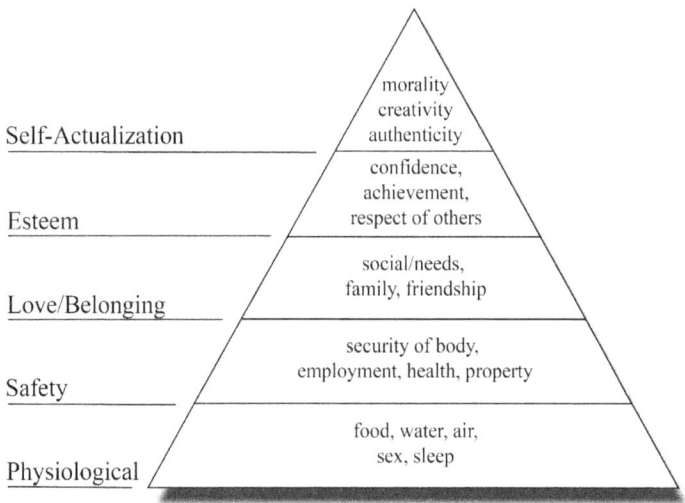

Maslow's Hierarchy of Needs

Core Needs. However, one cannot progress to the next level until the needs of the prior level are fulfilled. For example, you are unlikely to be able to focus on loving intimacy if you are starving or afraid of being killed.

You will notice that while you can meet some of these needs on your own, others require other people to fulfill. We are, as Aristotle pointed out, social animals. Most of us in America can find clean water to drink (for now, anyway), but we need other people for friendship, family, and loving intimacy.

What of your basic physical needs? Some people find it easy to work enough to supply food, shelter, and clothing, while others, pregnant or nursing mothers for instance, might need the financial support of a partner or the government.

What is important is that you assess yourselves honestly rather than believing you *should* be at a higher level.

Exercise: Where would you place yourself on Maslow's Hierarchy of Needs? Are you struggling to keep a roof over your head? To feed your family? Do you feel safe in your relationship and life? Or are you fearful of walking outside at night? Do you feel a sense of belonging in your family and circle of friends? Do you feel good about yourself and your achievements—or do you believe that others don't respect you?

Where do you think your partner is? Ask your partner—and share how you each feel about where you are right now. What do you learn?

Acceptance of the facts is a primary quality of the very highest level. Once you accept where you are, you can devise strategies to fulfill your needs at that level and build a solid foundation to move up the pyramid, one step at a time. Which of these needs can you meet for yourself? Which do you need others to meet? Please take a few minutes to consider these questions.

Other Needs

While Maslow's Hierarchy is perhaps the most famous model of human needs, you may find that he left out some that are important to you. Ashley Montague, among others, was a firm believer in the need for people to have play and laughter in their lives. I absolutely agree, as you will see when we get to the chapter on that subject. If you have a need that I don't cover, that doesn't mean it's not legitimate. A substantial portion of the world's population has a need to halt whatever they are doing and to pray toward Mecca five times a day. Other people wouldn't miss bathing in the Ganges at dawn every day. I had one client who needed to wrap himself up in athletic tape every few weeks. If you need something, you need it. You don't have to apologize for it or develop a rationalization worthy of a Supreme Court brief to defend it. What is most helpful is to honestly appraise what you need and to strategize how you can get most of a large portion of your needs met.

So long as what you need doesn't injure anyone or the planet—and the vast majority of human needs comply with that proviso—what could be wrong with attempting to get a need met? Obviously, I'm not talking about a damaging need—to molest children or to steal old folks' retirement accounts or purposefully cut yourself, for instance. Such hurtful needs need to be addressed in therapy.

However, a central problem in most relationships is that people assume that they will need to surrender their needs at the door in order to make the relationship work. That is a very dangerous assumption that too often kills the relationship rather than enhancing it. Please hear me: *Relationship is not about diminishing ourselves but about expanding ourselves.*

Remember Ken and Kathy? After their baby was born their energies switched, as often happens for couples with a new child, from their relationship being primary to the need to care for the baby. In fact, Ma Nature programs that in: Testosterone levels in Dad as well as Mom tend to fall and estrogen levels rise as the emphasis shifts to caring for an infant. It's then easy to neglect your love life and assume that dropping or minimizing sex is "normal." In one sense it is. At that point Ma Nature is much more interested in the well-being of the infant that she is in the quality of your relationship.

I notice that people tend to go to extremes at this point. One couple will drop sex entirely and become attentive parents. Another will farm the kid out with a nanny and begin attending four parties every week. Neither end of the pole is helpful to either relationship or, in fact, to children.

Children need attentive parents, yes, but they also need parents who have juice for one another. One of the greatest gifts parents can give a child is the example and ambience of their own warm, loving relationship. When Ken was expressing his need for that to her, a big part of Kathy knew that she had overbalanced away from him.

The issue here is balance. Both Ken and Kathy had a strong need to be attentive, loving parents. Both also had a strong need to have a passionate relationship. But they got polarized, with Kathy moving into the former role and Ken having to the reassert the latter. Rather than making one another wrong or bad about their primary need, however, they found a way to rebalance the polarity and meet *both* needs.

Needs are not necessarily unilateral. Often they are counterweighted by another or even several other needs. In addition to their needs to parent and keep their relationship vivid, Ken and Kathy had the need to work to make enough money to keep a roof over their heads and food on the table. They also felt a need to be active members of their church. Balancing out needs can be quite complex.

Nevertheless, you cannot balance what isn't put into the scales. You must identify your needs accurately and express them to your partner clearly. Then and only then can the work of finding balance among them begin.

Relationship Needs

Dr. Willard Harley, Jr., has broken down our relationship needs into some sub-categories that are helpful to consider.[6] In his long career as a marriage counselor in Minnesota he has found that the top five for men and the top five for women tend to be different. Take a guess at which column below is favored by which gender:

Affection	Sexual Fulfillment
Conversation	Recreational Companionship
Honesty & Openness	An Attractive Spouse
Financial Support	Domestic Support
Family Commitment	Admiration

If you guessed that women tend to favor the first column and men the second, you know some of the same people that Dr. Harley knows. I think the categories are fairly obvious from his labels for them, but if you have any questions about them don't hesitate to get his book or check out his website at <www.marriagebuilders.com>.

I would clarify that by "Family Commitment" is meant not only showing up for your partner and children, but also for your extended families. "Domestic Support" means such activities as getting the meals on the table and doing the laundry.

Which are your top five? Mine include affection, conversation, and honesty from the traditionally "feminine" side. What are your partner's? You might want to discuss the

---

6   *His Needs, Her Needs: Building an Affair-Proof Marriage* (2001).

similarities and differences that you discover, after you do the following exercise:

Exercise: List your needs as you are aware of them right now. Begin with where you are on Maslow's hierarchy. Write that need across the top of your paper and place a star beside it.

Next, write down your top five needs from Harley's list of ten, in order of importance to you.

Now, look over your list of needs and underline the ones that are currently being met. Circle the ones you really wish were being met.

If your partner is open to it, ask them to do this exercise. Then exchange lists.

What do you learn about yourself and your partner that you didn't know before?

The next step—a very important one—is to translate these general needs into specific actions that you each find doable.

Specific and Doable

When you ask to have a need met, put some thought into making it both specific and doable. For example, "I want you to show me more love" is not specific; "Make love with me ten times a day every day of the week" is probably not doable. "I would like to get naked and cuddle in bed and see what happens" is both specific and doable for most of us.

Sometimes it's difficult to take a generality (such as "I want more love") and to translate that into specific acts. *That is the job of the person who has the need.* As you clarify your needs you come to know yourself better. Don't be afraid to experiment: "We could try cuddling for ten minutes before we go to sleep and see if that works."

On the other hand, it's up to your partner to decide whether the specific task is doable. She can say, "Yes, I think I could do that. Let's try it for a week and see how it goes." Or she might say, "Not sure I can do that. Could we try just five minutes and see how I do with it?"

Later, we'll discuss how to negotiate so you each maximize the number of needs you are getting met. Right now, I encourage you to take your list of needs from the prior exercise and, for each general need, find at least one specific and (you hope) doable action that will manifest it, which we will do in the next exercise.

For example, I have a need for genuine admiration. Specifically, I like it when my partner notices when I have washed the cars or done the laundry and simply says, "I really appreciate your doing the laundry today." I really like it when she thanks me for giving her my undivided attention or negotiating with the phone company for a better rate. Please note: I am not asking for insincere flattery. What I want is to be recognized and appreciated for what I actually do and who I actually am. That works best when she grounds her appreciation in some specific action that she has witnessed me make. It's pleasant to hear "I think you're a wonderful man" but I get it at a deeper level when she adds "for protecting me from the rabid skunk."

Begin your list of specific and doable actions as follows:

Specific and doable: For each of your general needs, be it Maslow's need for love or Harley's need for affection, identify a specific act that you imagine your partner could do that would fill the more general need.

For example, if you have a need for affection, you might like your partner to manifest that in some of the following ways:

1. I'd like to cuddle for 5 minutes after we wake up in the morning.
2. I'd like us to share a hug and a kiss before leaving for work.
3. I'd like to trade 15 minute massages once a week with you.

Jot down as many specifics as you can for as many needs as you can in 5 or 10 minutes. (You can always return to this list later.) Now, review your list and rate each specific action from 1 to 10, with a 1 meaning "This carries some positive charge" and a 10 means "Wadonda!"

Next, give your list to your partner and ask whether what you are asking for is clear enough and doable. Then, ask whether he or she would like to give you their own list.

You now each have in hand a list of specific and doable acts that you *know* will communicate directly with your partner's deepest needs. When you wish to do so, you can refer to their list and select such an act that will help you connect at a deeper level.

But What Happens When My Partner Just Won't Go There?

Most people I've counseled are *delighted* to have a list of specific ways to meet their partner's needs. The biggest problem in most coupleships is that neither partner has a clear idea of how to do so and both have become frustrated when their best guesstimates aren't doing the job. Most of us want to please our partners and having specific guidelines on precisely how to do so is a huge relief.

If, however, a partner is totally uninterested in doing anything on your list, your relationship is in serious jeopardy. I would suggest you get it into counseling immediately.

That having been said, most of us will probably find one or two items on our partner's list undoable.

What you can do is to say, for instance, "I see that you'd like it very much (an 8!) if I would take sole responsibility for putting the kids to bed every night. While I'm not willing to do so every night, I'd be happy to do it four nights a week." In other words, acknowledge your partner's wish and make a counter-proposal that *is* doable for you.

However, if he says, "I just can't go there," you will need to deal with your disappointment and find a substitute behavior that works for you. But, ultimately, you will have to organize around not having every need met by your partner. Here's an important truth that every relationship must confront and learn to organize around:

No one other human being can meet
all of your needs.

Adrian came in yesterday disappointed that his partner was uninterested in discussing life on a philosophical level with him.

"I love to have a good, mind-expanding argument about the basic nature of life, the universe, and everything," he said. "She's totally uninterested. She's a down-to-earth, practical girl. She wants to talk about the kids or what the dog did today. So it goes nowhere."

I pointed out that this was a need he could meet with friends who were similarly inclined without endangering the relationship.

"Yeah, but I'm still bummed. I want it all with one person."

"You would like to have it all with one person," I said, "and what's the reality?"

"Yeah, yeah, I know, I know."

The fact is that none of us will have all of our needs met by one partner. That expectation—that one person will meet all our needs all the time—is unreal, and it causes an enormous amount of pain and frustration in relationships. Which needs can you meet for yourself and which will you need others to meet, without jeopardizing the relationship?

There are a couple of priority grids here. First, I must learn to identify my needs and to ask my partner to fill those that she indicates are doable. Second, I will have to find means to fill those she doesn't find doable, as Adrian might fill his need for philosophical discussion with friends. Third, I will need to keep a weather eye open to the fact that I might be growing closer to my philosopher friends than my partner and to assess whether the fact that my partner doesn't want to fill this need is a deal-breaker. (Outside of sexuality, that is seldom the case. Obviously, if my partner wants an active sex life and I'm uninterested in that, we'll have a major problem to negotiate very carefully.)

Obstacles to Identifying Needs

The first step is to identify our needs. There are a number of obstacles to doing so. Let's examine them each in turn so we can figure out ways to circumvent the obstacles.

The most challenging obstacle is the one we just examined: Being general rather than specific. Notice that both Maslow's and Harley's lists of needs are pretty general. However, we do not live our lives *generally* but in the specific details. Unfortunately, we often think and speak in generalities, such as "We are a generous nation" rather than the more specific "We distributed over a million bushels of wheat to India during their last famine." It's easier, and lazier, to live in generalities than in the actualities of our lives—until we hit a crunch point where we find that only the actual is true and that we have been deluding ourselves and our partners. Generalities are castles in the air; we must connect them to the ground with a scaffolding of specific details. In addition to your List of Needs from the previous exercises, a simple way to do so is to observe the specific actions that you and your partner make that trigger a loving feeling in you, as in the "I feel loving when…" exercise from p. 124 of *Real Relationship*. Take a few minutes to notice the parallels between the two.

Does having a need met by a specific act help
you feel more loving?

There are several other obstacles to identifying our needs.

Some people have trouble acknowledging that they have needs at all. Often they had to take care of themselves from a very early age. Part of doing so meant they had to dampen down their awareness of the needs and wishes they were unlikely to have met. I know this tendency well. Growing up in a large family with two working parents who struggled to feed us, pay the mortgage, and send us to good schools, I knew better than to ask for a new bicycle for my seventh birthday. Instead, I cut other people's lawns to make the five dollars it took to buy a chum's old bike. I loved that bike. As an adult, I had to do a lot of work to learn how to admit to myself that I had *any* needs.

To counteract this obstacle, you will need to become mindful of your real needs. Some people can do so simply by continually asking themselves, "What do I want now?" Others, like me, will need to do some therapy to remove the blockages to admitting our needs to ourselves.

At the opposite end of the spectrum, some people are constantly needy, asking for help (or playing helpless) in situations that they could manage perfectly well on their own. There was a time when women needed men to open doors or light cigarettes for them. And there are still men who can't seem to find the hamper, much less do the wash. Excessive neediness of this sort will tend to turn off people who would otherwise wish to meet your needs. The corrective is to assess yourself for learned helplessness and to develop a program for learning to do those things that an average adult can do. That includes doing the wash, folding the clothes, and putting them into the proper places. It also includes being able to check the oil in the car and add a quart, when needed.

Some people have a great deal of difficulty in grasping the fact that their partner is not just like them. If I hate washing the dishes and do that for my partner because it's what I'd like her to do for me, I will be flabbergasted to discover that she *loves* washing dishes and was letting me do so (for three years!) only because she thought I loved it as much as she. So the first step, after identifying your relationship needs, is to be able to share them with your partner honestly and have your partner understand these important parts of you.

Some people shrink from this step. They don't want to ask to have a need met. They hope that their partner will be able to intuit their needs and meet them without having to be asked to do so. As babies, we all needed parents who could intuit our needs. Some of us want to remain infants whose partners will be the perfect Mommy or Daddy we never had, in actuality. When the partner fails to meet this high expectation, as will inevitably happen, we will be as frustrated with them as a hungry child is with a clueless caregiver.

Try This: For one week, observe yourself carefully for when you want something but avoid asking for it. Notice what you do instead: Do you pout and hope your partner will read your mind and provide it for you? Do you just try to take care of it yourself? Do you attempt to get the need met elsewhere?

Can you observe yourself compassionately, without judgment? With gentle curiosity? Or do you find yourself being harshly critical of yourself?

What do you need to do about that?

It is each individual's job to identify and then to communicate what he or she wishes/needs in relationship, in very specific terms. Ken was doing that when he set the session and told Kathy that he wanted them to have a better sexual relationship. As you begin to identify your wishes and needs and to communicate them to your partner, observe what happens inside you.

Observing Yourself

Socrates said "The unexamined life is not worth living." While that might be a bit of an overstatement, it certainly dramatizes the idea. Learning how to observe yourself compassionately is one of the keys to happiness. By doing so, you develop that part of your consciousness which stands outside of your thoughts, feelings, and actions. That part of us usually has one of two tones: Critical and Compassionate. The Critical Observer is easy to identify. It is a negative faultfinder who says things like, "You are so dumb to think that—and such a coward to be afraid. Oh no, that was the worst thing you could have done." The Critical Observer tends to make us feel terrible. It is not what I mean when I suggest you observe yourself. When you hear yourself deriding yourself in this way, change the disc. Take out the Critical Observer cacophony and insert the Compassionate Observer melody.

The Compassionate Observer is the part of our minds that can notice what we are thinking, feeling, and doing with acceptance and kindness. This part of us simply observes without judgment or moralizing, saying things like, "Of course it's scary to tell your partner what you need. How do you feel in your body when you put yourself down like that?"

Having been raised in a moralistic, post-Puritan culture that lays a lot of *shoulds* and *shalt-nots* upon us, most Americans judge themselves and others harshly, expecting a level of perfection that is not human. We can come to know the possible human by observing ourselves as we actually are— which is sometimes challenging when we discover that our basic humanity is fraught with contradictions and can often be less than stellar.

Just yesterday I heard on my local NPR station a research psychologist named David DeSteno describing a fascinating experiment designed to reveal what we call "character," which we assume to be constant. In fact, he and his research partner, Piercarlo Valdesolo, found that people often act "out of character"—and then rationalize their behavior.

DeSteno and Valdesolo asked volunteers to flip a coin to choose between one of two tasks—a five-minute fun task or an hour-long boring one—knowing that the next volunteer would have to do the undone task. Believing they were unobserved, 90% of the volunteers skipped the coin flip and did the quick, fun task. Later, when the researchers asked them whether they'd acted fairly, they lied and said they had.[7]

But here's the best part: When the researchers then had them observe a "volunteer" (actually an actor) do exactly what they had done—skip the coin flip and do the short task—they *almost universally condemned the actor.*

------

7   See their book, *Out of Character: Surprising Truths About the Liar, Cheat, Sinner (and Saint) Lurking in All of Us* (2011).

Sound familiar? We humans tend to rationalize our actions and then to hypocritically *judge others who act the very same way*. It is therefore difficult for us to observe ourselves objectively and compassionately. Our capacities for delusion ("I wouldn't cheat like that!") and denial ("I didn't actually cheat…") are monumental.

I can't tell you how many times I have heard people in my consulting room say something like a demure woman I'll call Priscilla did after she had hit her husband: "That's not me. I don't hit people." Her self-concept was clearly at odds with what she had just done, so much so that she found it difficult to acknowledge her behavior. When the dissonance between the behavior and the self-concept is uncomfortable enough, people will "forget" the actual behavior. "Oh, no, I never hit him. I would never do such a thing."

One way we can begin to break down our tendency to continue to live in such unreality is to watch how we think and act, without judgment. I suggest that you imagine you are an anthropologist from another galaxy who is studying human beings and observe yourself with that kind of objectivity. This will require courage, because we will find that we don't live up to our expectations of how we should be. Admitting that to ourselves isn't easy. But it is the beginning of becoming real rather than deluded people.

Real people can have real relationships.

Treat Your Partner the Same Way

As you develop your skill in observing yourself with kind compassion and loving acceptance, you will hone your capacity to do the same with your partner. Observe her or him with the same lovingkindness that you practice with yourself. Keep replacing your expectations of how your partner *should* be with accurate observations of how he or she is.

Kimberley was quite unhappy that Jack couldn't remember those significant dates, such as their anniversary and her birthday. At least twice a year she'd get the blues when the date passed without a card or a flower. Finally she realized that Jack was date-challenged and that her punishing moods didn't manipulate him into remembering. She knew that she had a need for him to celebrate the dates—so she began reminding him a few days ahead of the day.

"Honey, our anniversary is Saturday. You know how much it means to me to celebrate it in some way. Can we go out to dinner at Friar Tuck's Saturday night? I'd love it if you'd write me a romantic note of some kind and slip it to me during dinner."

Asking for what she wanted was challenging for Kim. She wanted to feel special by having her partner keep track of important dates religiously. But careful observation taught her that Jack wasn't going to do that. So she could feel awful twice a year, become blue and pull away, then unload on him when he asked what was the matter—*or she could come up with a plan to get what she wanted by asking for it directly*—a few days in advance.

Once thus reminded, Jack was happy to write her a love sonnet (he was quite the poet) and enjoy a romantic dinner out. Kim found that, while it wasn't her perfect fantasy of how her partner was supposed to be, she could actually enjoy herself rather than spend days in a funk.

For his part, Jack was sad that Kim almost never initiated love-making with him. He craved a partner who came on to him like a randy wench. When he finally admitted to Kim that this was the case, she said that she'd been brought up to believe that a woman who did so was a slut.

"Fantastic!" Jack said. "I'd love you to be a slut—with me!"

He went on to give her a few specifics about his idea of a great slut.

The next day when Jack came home from work, Kim met him at the front door wearing only a drop of perfume and greeted him with a kiss that knocked his shoes off.

Jack was grinning from ear to ear at their next session, and Kim looked like the cat that had swallowed the canary.

"I'm loving my inner slut," she said. "Jack has created a monster."

Listen Carefully to Your Partner's Needs

You will need to ask about and to hear your partner's needs. Be sure to mirror back what you hear.[8] Then either say you believe you can meet that need and will embark upon a two-week trial—or enter into negotiation to find something that will work for both of you.

Never disparage your partner's needs. Take them very seriously indeed, even if you do not fully understand them. The fact that you don't understand them does not mean they aren't valid or important to your partner. When needs

---

8   Please review Chapter 6 ("Listen!") in *Real Relationship*.

are disparaged, that partner is then likely to be soon telling someone else those classic words, "My partner doesn't understand me...."

Anything other than acknowledgement and acceptance of your partner's needs is a form of disparagement. Oftentimes, one partner will try to reason another out of a need, as in, "You know, dear, I can give you ten good reasons why you shouldn't have that need." Please understand that many of our needs may seem unreasonable, even to ourselves. That doesn't make them one iota less real.

Many men, being less verbal,[9] will disparage a woman's need to feel close through conversation. Many women will disparage a man's wish to watch or play sports. The fact that one person doesn't "get" the other's need does not make that need any less important, and the disparagement injures the relationship.

Please remember that the fact that something is not your cup of tea doesn't mean that your partner might not need it. I am gregarious and really enjoy getting together with friends frequently. Yashi is more inward and needs time to herself in quiet. This extrovert/introvert polarity was one of the first of the character traits to be identified by psychologists. It's probably genetic in origin. It can be a source of misunderstanding and friction in relationship. Some partners will see their opposite as "weird" and try to change them. Yashi could say that I am a social butterfly. I could say she's a bit of a hermit. Fortunately for us, neither of us has ever said or even thought such things. We understand and accept this basic difference.

---

9   According to Louann Brizendine in *The Female Brain* (2006), men average 7000 words per day, women 20.000.

Each of us is also aware of our own inner polarity: There is a big part of me that really treasures quiet. There is a big part of Yashi that really enjoys getting together with people. What we do is to negotiate a balance between these needs in our mutual life, and then augment that for our own individual needs. For example, we will sit down with our monthly calendar and pick a couple of times to get together with friends. In counterbalance, we also designate one day a week as "Soul Day."

Soul Day

Soul Day is one day each week during which we relate minimally and each of us does our own thing. After we share dreams in the morning over breakfast, we don't speak again to each other until the following morning. Yashi likes to spend the day alone. She will meditate, play her flute, and go for long walks in Nature. I will nourish my soul by playing a sport with my buddies and then enjoying a good tailgate party that often includes adult beverages and some crude jokes that provoke mindless mirth. Or I might go to an action movie with a friend.

As you can see, what's most important is that each one of us knows and accepts ourselves—and each other—and asks for what we want.

Soul Day is that time each week when we create an interlude from our relating and do those things which our own souls crave. We then re-experience what it was like to be a separate being. It provides a refreshing break—and we're eager to reconnect the following day.

The important point is that we don't have a delusion that our relationship will meet all of our needs. We are clear that it will not and that some of those needs are best met individually. Fine, you say, but what about those needs that are relational? What if my partner doesn't want to meet my need for, say, conversation, to the extent that I wish it?

Remember the Golden Rule

While it is important for each partner to understand that "you can't always get what you want," as the Rolling Stones sing, and to be able to work through the painful feelings that will come up if you can't get your way, what would you like to hear when you tell your partner about a need you have? I am much more likely to be able to let go of my hurt feelings when my partner does not respond to my wish with an "Absolutely not!" but rather with something more like "I'm sorry I can't meet that need. Is there something else I could do for you that would make you happy?" Her willingness to try to meet my needs goes a long way.

The Golden Rule is useful here:

Jesus said: "Do unto others as you would have them do unto you." Confucius said: "Do not do to others what you wouldn't like done to you."

I would like my partner to hear my wishes and to meet them if she can. I want to know hers and to meet them if I can. If she's asking for something I just don't want to do, I can gently say that, without judgment, and negotiate a workable alternative. I would like the same kind consideration from her.

A possible confusion sometimes comes up around this wonderful rule. Because we are not clones of one another, what one person wants is not necessarily what another would like. As you may remember, Yashi would love it if I cooked Brussels sprouts for her, while I would think she was trying to poison me if she were to cook them for me. Part of how I would like others to treat me *is to be aware that I am a separate person with different needs.*

I made this mistake one Christmas when I got Yashi what I thought would be a terrific gift—a Daisy air rifle. Since that day, when I showed her how to load and shoot it, I don't think she's touched it. When I thought about it, I realized that my gift to her wasn't really about her but about me: I'd given her what I wanted. When I was a boy my parents refused to let me have a Daisy air rifle on the supremely logical grounds that a BB gun could foster a careless attitude toward weapons, since it was unlikely that you could kill or even seriously maim another with one. They made me wait till I was eleven, when they got me a twenty-two caliber Winchester rifle and my father taught me gun safety.

I think they were right, because my buddies, who all had Daisies, would shoot at each other with them, until one of them got hit in the eye. (Miraculously, the BB entered the eye socket and then came out his nose a day later, leaving the eyeball undamaged. He survived to become a policeman.) Nevertheless, I longed for a Daisy as a boy—and finally got one, disguised as a gift for Yashi.

But what happens when your partner wishes for something that you judge as positively "weird"? Though it's fairly easy for most people to ask for a neck rub or five minute's attention, most of us have some needs that we feel embarrassed about divulging, because we judge them as not "normal." After working in this field for going on four decades, I can honestly say that human beings are capable of just about anything imaginable. Some of what we are capable of is cruel or destructive, which, obviously, we must learn to control. On the other hand there are countless behaviors that people enjoy that, while not being widespread, do not hurt anyone. If something gives you pleasure and isn't hurting anyone or the planet, what harm is there in it?

Religious Proscriptions

Into this category fall many of the ancient religious proscriptions. I find it interesting that if some strange rule is part of a religion we seem to give it automatic sanction, even if it seems nuts to us. Both Islam and Judaism prohibit the eating of pork, while most Americans gobble tons of the "other white meat." Catholicism used to mandate regular fish eating. I can remember how exotic it was for me, as a lad, to eat at a Catholic friend's house on a Friday and to be served fish. We almost never ate fish at my table unless we'd caught it ourselves that day.

An Israeli psychologist devised an instructive questionnaire that demonstrated that a huge majority of Israeli schoolchildren thought that Joshua was right to slay everyone in Jericho. (You remember, "Joshua fit the battle of Jericho...and the walls came tumblin' down.") When, in the control group, students were confronted with a parallel scenario that had a Chinese General Ling slaughtering the citizens of a rival Mongol city, the children overwhelmingly (85%) judged him as wrong to do so. It is no surprise that people bound by the groupthink of a particular religion might be challenged to think outside that box. That is one of the reasons many religions insist that devotees marry within the religion—there are more challenges to a "religiously mixed" coupleship. Mark Twain tells an amusing story in his *Autobiography* of the time he and John Hay were having an enjoyable gabfest, augmented with cigars, when Mr. Hay's wife returned from church and the temperature in the room dropped by fifty degrees. When she had retired, a rather peaked John Hay said, "She is somewhat particular about the Sabbath."[10]

It's easy to poke fun at someone else's beliefs if we don't share them. Yet we have come to honor others' religious beliefs, however strange they might seem to us, so long as the true believers don't attempt to impose them upon us. In the same way, we can honor our partner's needs, even if we don't fully understand them.

The Man Who Loved Feet

All of us hold similar prejudices in the same way as the Israeli schoolchildren or Mrs. Hay and will benefit from broadening our perspectives. The following experience helped me stretch a bit.

One of my clients really loved women's feet. He liked to examine them, touch them, and kiss them. His wife judged

---

10   *Autobiography of Mark Twain*, vol. 1, H.E. Smith, editor (2010).

him "weird" and pushed him into therapy. Though I knew that what the literature calls a "foot fetish" is actually fairly widespread—for centuries the Chinese bound the feet of girls to inhibit their growth, for example—I couldn't say that I had an intuitive grasp of why someone would be fixated on that particular part of the human body. A part of me judged it as odd, I blush to admit.

What I do know is that how we are wired is not whimsical but has some internal logic to it that, once understood, makes perfect sense. There is a French expression which, loosely translated, says, "To understand is to forgive."

My client was in distress because he judged himself as weird as his wife said he was and because he hated to disappoint her. He wanted me to help him excise his love of feet.

When he stayed with the feeling of longing that he had for a woman's foot, he found himself traveling back in time to his early days of babyhood. His father had abandoned the family when he was a baby. His mother didn't hold him much. To make ends meet, she worked hard every day at home as a seamstress, sewing buttons onto people's shirts and altering slacks. To her credit, she did not lock him away in some closet but kept him with her in her workspace, where he crawled around on the floor while she worked. The part of his mother that he could see and touch were her feet, as they rocked the cradle of the sewing machine. He bonded more with her feet than any other part of her.

After he relived this early memory, we both understood why he might be attached to women's feet. More importantly, he could accept that, given this experience, of course he would love his wife's feet. Thirdly, he discovered that his formerly powerful attachment to them had somewhat mitigated.

In the next session he brought his wife in with him and explained to her, with a bit of help from me, why he found a woman's feet so alluring. When I asked her to mirror back to him what she was hearing him say, she seemed to relax a little bit. They then went on to talk about how they might incorporate some foot play into their relationship in a way that she wouldn't be uncomfortable with.

A few weeks later she came in on her own to work with her difficulty in accepting being adored. She realized her husband really adored all of her, not just her feet, and that because she had never been cherished as a child she was uncomfortable with it.

What I find in most couple interactions is that there is often a perfect fit between their issues. He adored her feet, she was uneasy with adoration. He wanted her to accept him, she thought him weird. It's as if each of our unconscious minds has purposefully selected *this* partner who is guaranteed to bring our old pain into the light of our love.

If we continue to bury some part of ourselves, it will fester. If we bring it up into the light of our love, we can let it be loved. Remember: You don't need to explain or justify your needs. As Shakespeare put it succinctly, "Reason not the need." Hopefully, you and your partner will honor one another's needs simply because they belong to a loved one.

Give Each Other Insider Information

Once you are sharing your needs and wishes with each other and have handed each other a list detailing your needs, you are well on your way to being open and honest in your relationship, which is another fundamental building block in any good, long-term, intimate relationship. We will turn to honesty in the next chapter.

As we learn to meet each other's needs, mindfully and thoughtfully, we forestall the lightning-quick subcortical reactivity of the human brain with its tendency to perceive a threat where there is in fact none. We have descended from a long line of people who were hypersensitive to the possibility that a saber-toothed tiger was behind every tree. Potential ancestors who were less anxious tended to be lunch for such tigers. The more paranoid survived to procreate. So we carry time-tested genes that alert us to even the remote possibility of a threat—an advantage in the jungle red in tooth and claw but a major problem in the home.

On the other hand, when we meet each other's needs, at least some of the time, the opposite happens: We trigger the flow of oxytocin, the bonding hormone, and we feel safe and relaxed. Other primates engage in this behavior when they groom one another. You might have experienced a warm, friendly feeling when your hairdresser massages your scalp and makes your coiffure just so. Or when you receive a massage. (I suggest that couples trade hair-washings and massages.) And what is most likely to trigger oxytocin is when your partner has gotten to know over time what you need and is able to offer it to you before you even ask. Remember: If you *expect* your partner to meet your needs without you having to ask, you will create a lot of pain for yourself. If we don't expect it and it then happens, we get a real boost.

Here's a very basic example. Yashi has figured out that when I haven't eaten in a while I can get grumpy. So after I've had a long day and I'm still in my office writing reports and making phone calls, she'll appear like an angel to bring me a snack, maybe just some cheese and crackers or a few cashews. Interestingly, I usually don't even have any awareness that I'm hungry, but I notice that the snack tastes great and that I immediately start feeling better.

In this case, she wasn't working off of my List of Needs but from her own intuition—and it turned out she was right. She had spotted and then filled a need that I didn't even know I had.

However, sometimes what you think *must* be a partner's need actually isn't. In that case, your partner must be honest with you and tell you so, gently, while appreciating your effort, and you'll have to face the fact that you misperceived him or her. That's okay; you just got to understand your partner a little bit better—and he or she knows your heart is in the right place.

I cannot count the number of coupleships I have worked with in which one person was working hard to meet a need that the other actually didn't have—but saying nothing for fear of hurting their partner's feelings. One man had, for 35 years, been pushing himself out of bed earlier than he wished to make the coffee and bring his wife a cup in bed. Until the therapy session, she couldn't bring herself to tell him that, when she was single, one of her greatest pleasures was to get up early, put on the coffee, and sit alone in the morning sun with her hands wrapped around a warm cup reading the newspaper.

"When you beat me up that first day," she said, "and brought me coffee, I was so touched that I couldn't tell you it wasn't really what I wanted—and I'm awfully embarrassed to say that I've been afraid to bring it up for all these years."

Her husband laughed.

"It's a real chore for me," he said. "I only did it because I thought you liked it."

They agreed that he could sleep in and she'd get up, make the coffee, and read the paper. Then she'd bring him a cup in bed, which is what he'd really wanted all along.

We will often do for others what we'd like them to do for us. Check out what you're doing for your partner or parent and ask yourself "Would I like it if someone were doing this for me?" That's a simple way to uncover unconscious needs.

Don't assume that your good services are truly appreciated. Check it out with your partner—and encourage him or her to be honest.

When we are working from the more reliable information on our partner's List, they will tend to forget the fact that they have thoughtfully provided us with which specific acts are most likely to trigger their loving feelings. When you want to show your partner some love, get out his or her List or "I feel loving when…" sheet and find a specific and doable action that you can perform which is likely to spark oxytocin.

It works. Try it. It fills up your partner's Love Bank.

Fill Up Your Partner's Love Bank

When my partner is attentive to me and wishes to meet my needs, I will feel warmly toward her. It's as if each time she meets a need she makes a deposit in the account in my internal love bank that has her name on it.

When she does something that hurts or annoys me, she withdraws some of that credit.

Each of us carries within us an unconscious account that credits need-meeting with positive credits and deprivation or hurts with withdrawals—for every person in our lives. We look forward to being with those with whom we have a big credit and we will begin to avoid those who are deep in the red with us.

How can we fill our partner's love bank *consciously* so that she or he will want to be around us? Quite simply, by identifying his or her needs and then meeting them as frequently as we reasonably can.

At the beginning of a romance, there are usually enormous deposits of positive credits in the love bank, for at this stage, while we are high on the Love Cocktail, we not only willingly give generously to a partner but also tend to interpret his or her acts in a very positive light. But as time goes on, and the Love Cocktail wanes, two things happen: We become less attentive and we will tend to interpret some of the very same acts in a negative light.

Mary, who was a bit shy, found Tim's outgoing personality very attractive when they met. She admired how he could strike up conversations with anyone and connect with them easily. Yet when they came in for couples counseling her primary complaint was that Tim seemed more interested in other people than he was in her.

For his part, Tim had found Mary's shyness extremely endearing. He used to say of her, "Still waters run deep." But two years later he found her to be a stick-in-the-mud.

Same qualities, different interpretations.

This often happens with couples. The very quality that they once found so attractive in their partner now seems an irritant.

When partners are looking at each other with an irritated, critical eye rather than an adoring one, of course they both feel badly. They believe they have "fallen out of love." The withdrawals from the previously credit-rich love bank are hemorrhaging the account. Soon the account is deeply in the red—and the partners are seeing red. Or just yawning.

> *There is a very simple antidote: Reverse the outflow of credits by consciously meeting your partner's needs when you can do so and thereby pouring positive credit into the love bank, remembering that no one can fill all of anyone's needs but that filling some of them creates love.*

The very fact that Tim was willing to come into counseling with Mary and pay close attention to her in that setting began the process. When she could tell him how much she valued his doing so, he, too, received positive credits. Together, they set up some structured ways to make sure they set aside time each day to meet each other's needs. Because they'd caught the problem early, it didn't take long for them to fall back in love again.

Please take this truth to heart: *You can re-create loving feelings together simply by filling some of each other's needs.*

Needs Can Change Over Time

On a regular basis—and at least once a year—ask your partner to give you both your "I feel loving when" and your core needs lists back for you to review. Read them over, asking yourself, "Is this still a need of mine? Is the number I have assigned to it still appropriate? Have I moved up Maslow's pyramid? Is there anything I wish to change or add?"

You will probably notice that many of your needs are the same as they were, while a few have a different value to you and some might have become obsolete. When I was a teen-ager, several of my girlfriends remarked that I seemed to have a one-track mind. I replied that, being so sex-starved, I didn't have a mind at all. I was stuck at Maslow's bottom level. Once I was in a good sexual relationship, however, I could then focus on other aspects of mind and heart. Have you had a similar experience of being able to move up the pyramid?

Doing your yearly review with your partner might well trigger perceptions of new needs that you have developed. You will find this yearly review illuminating for yourself, and your partner will appreciate the update.

When she has done her review of her list at the same time, you can then sit down together and share your changes, bringing each other up to date and reminding yourselves of the importance of meeting each other's needs as often as you can.

Timing

When you meet your partner's need might be even more important than how you meet it. For example, Yashi has confided that when I meet her needs for attention and conversation first thing in the morning, even a brief ten or fif-teen minutes can fill her up for the whole day. When she has to wait for it, she can get grumpy.

Of course, I am just the opposite: I like to start the morning slowly and inwardly. It's the time I write best. So it isn't easy for me to push myself into attending to her for even so short a time. However, the results of my doing so are so positive that I keep doing it. The small sacrifice I make by varying my own morning ritual to include showering her with fifteen minutes of loving attention pays huge dividends in our relationship. She makes us hot lemon water and we sit watching the birds come to the feeders outside our sliding glass door and share our dreams of the night before, checking in on how we each feel.

Then we share a hug and I go to my study to write.

Timing is sometimes situational as well. Doug complained to his partner June that while she was very affectionate in public she was seldom so at home. He said that the paranoid story he made up was that she would hold and kiss him in public as a means of claiming him as her territory, to ward off other women.

June thought about that story for a minute or so, then said, "I don't think you're being totally paranoid. I think there's a large nugget of truth in what you're saying. Certainly I'm more aware of wanting to be close with you in public. But I do really like being affectionate with you and I'll be more conscious of showing you more affection at home."

Summary

We all have wishes and needs that we ignore or discount at our peril. When we become conscious of them, we can then share them openly with our partner. When we write our needs down it gives the partner a list of specific and doable actions that will trigger our loving feelings toward him or her and add credits to the love bank. We will need to overcome our infantile hope that our partner will be able to discern our needs and meet them without our having to communicate them. We will also have to accept the fact that no one person will be able to meet all of our needs all of the time.

Clarify for yourself which of your needs you can meet on your own or with friends and which you would like your partner to meet. Ask directly to have those needs met, while understanding that no partner is going to be the perfect Mommy or Daddy you never had. If he or she can't or won't meet a need, grieve that disappointment and then do what you can to meet the need yourself, in a way that doesn't injure the relationship.

At the same time, ask your partner to divulge his or her needs to you, and work to meet them as often and as fully as you can, within the limits of your capacity. Accept your limits, and those of your partner. Focus on the valuable gifts you are getting from the relationship rather than on what you lack.

Work to keep your own and your partner's love banks richly in the black and you will find that your relationship thrives.

CHAPTER 2:
BE OPEN AND HONEST WITH EACH OTHER

Honesty is the best policy.
—Ben Franklin

Why do I need to write a chapter about honesty being effective when Ben Franklin articulated that truth over 200 years ago? And while Franklin placed his famous aphorism in the context of good business practice, I believe it applies to our loving relationships as well. Isn't that apparent to everyone? Don't we all have a need for our partners to be honest with us? Aren't we open and honest with them?

The short answer is no. Seldom are partners open and honest with each other. As TV's Dr. House maintains, "Everyone lies," and there is considerable research that backs him up.[11] We tell ourselves we don't want to hurt our partner or that it's really only a "little white lie." We rationalize.

One of my clients pointed out that the word "rationalize" sounds and means the same as "rational lies."

So we are confronted with a very basic human paradox: On the one hand we all lie—to ourselves, to our partners, to our families, to our bosses, to the IRS. On the other, we live in a culture that has a very clear commandment ("Thou shalt not lie") and people like Ben Franklin admonishing us to be truthful for any number of reasons. The only way we

---

11   Baumeister & Tierney, *op. cit.*

can tolerate this paradox is by entering into a certain level of denial in which we tell ourselves that we don't *really* lie. That much. Or about important issues.

If we decide we want to co-create a lie-free relationship, we have to start by observing ourselves and acknowledging when we lie and when we are truthful—with compassionate curiosity. Doing so will be challenging at first, because there's a big part of us that doesn't want to admit our denial, even to ourselves. My suggestion is to observe yourself as a good cultural anthropologist from Mars might, without judgment but curious about what makes these Earthlings tick. Your compassionate Inner Observer can then notice, "Hmm. You just told a half-truth when you said you never ate chocolate. You ate a whole box of See's just last month."

Why is a lie-free relationship valuable? Two basic reasons: First, if I tell my partner a lie, she will then question anything I say, not being sure whether I might not be telling her another.

Once a lie is discovered it usually damages a relationship, even if it's just a "little white one." And lies have a way of being discovered.

Sometimes a relationship will unravel over a single lie that might seem petty to someone outside the couple. I knew one such couple who moved from being very much in love one minute to completely fractured the next when she found out that he had been lying to her about "friending" old flames on Facebook. "You told me you weren't going on it anymore!" she said. "If you lie to me about that, what else are you lying to me about? I'm totally out trust with you."

Her interesting phrase "out trust" pinpoints the core of the issue: Once we find that someone has lied to us we find it more difficult to trust anything that they say.

On the other hand, when we are as transparent as glass to our partners, revealing even—or especially—our dark sides, they can relax and feel safe with us, for they then *know* we are honest and open. At the same time, we can then relax into being transparently ourselves, without pretence, which is the second basic reason a lie-free relationship is a nice place to live. We can grow ourselves into people who feel better about who we are.

Transparency is absolutely necessary for a coupleship recovering from an affair. It is also one of the best ways to avoid one.

But let's not set up a rigid either-or polarity here, as in: We are either liars or truth-tellers. Human beings don't do well with such rigidities. Whenever we are working on improving ourselves, it is helpful to approach the process as a good baseball batter does: By improving our average. If I expect to get a hit every time I bat, I will be severely disappointed. If I work on getting one hit every three at bats rather than going one for four, I'll probably win the National League batting title.

Each time you are at that choice point where you can lie or tell the truth, you are standing at the plate. You don't have to hit a home run every time. Work on improving your average. Stay conscious and be compassionate with yourself. With practice, you'll find that you are speaking more truthfully and telling fewer fibs. As that happens, you'll find yourself feeling better about who you have become and you'll find your relationship blossoming.

But What About Mystery?

There is a widespread delusion that relationships need mystery to survive, that if we allow our partners to know us they will lose interest. I think the grain of truth in this belief is that it can seem to work for people who are addicted to struggling for love. It is true that some people just can't say no to a good, futile struggle, be it in relationship or a losing cause, and will jettison a good relationship that lacks struggle. They are of course never happy for very long. And what of their partners? If I buy into the idea that I must be mysterious, I must necessarily continually hide and dissemble myself and never be loved for who I actually am. To me, this sounds like a recipe for suffering. Besides, this preoccupation with superficial games overlooks the essential Mystery that is always present. Love will always surprise us.

However well we think we know our partners, there is at the core of each of us the Great Mystery of our essential divinity, which cannot be understood intellectually. We can only apprehend it through our feelings and intuition, and then stand in awe of it.

When I am as transparent as I can be, both to myself and to you, I open a way in to the deeper mystery of my being. I also grow myself into a person of greater integrity.

"Know Thyself"

"Know thyself" is a very ancient Greek injunction inscribed in the forecourt of the temple of Apollo at Delphi which is still pertinent today. If I don't know myself, how can I be open and honest with you? The better I know myself, the more clearly I can give you accurate information about me. The more I observe myself so I can tell you who I am, the better I know myself. It will be helpful for you to know about me that my musical tastes run to Mozart, Don Williams, and the Stones but veer away from rap or Chinese opera. If we are to be in close relationship, even as roommates, I want to know your likes and dislikes. Yashi introduced me to Dire Straits. If you don't know what you like, how can you expect me to intuit it?

Many young people begin relationships without having a clear sense of who they really are. The benefit is that they have more plasticity in their capacity to adapt to a partner. As they mature and determine what they like, they become less inclined to sacrifice some part of themselves for the apparent good of the relationship.

It is quite common for a young—or even just a new—couple to believe that they are remarkably similar. As we are bonding we will tend to see our similarities and not wish to inconvenience our partner with our differences. However, as the Love Cocktail wears off, our differences will come to the fore. Many couples incorrectly take this normal stage in relationship to mean they are falling out of love.

When Yashi and I were first getting to know each other, we were actually shocked by our remarkable similarities, such as bringing each other the same Rumi poem and an identical exotic rose to our first date. I cannot count the number of times we each said, "Gosh, we're so much alike!" in that first year. Everything went swimmingly and easily.

As our second year rolled around, what I heard increasingly from her was, "We're so *different*! I don't think we have anything in common!" I might have said it once or twice myself. Many parts of our relationship became challenging for us.

We joined an intensive couples' group with Pete Pearson and Ellyn Bader that met every day from nine to five for a week. Pete and Ellyn had written the book (*In Quest of the Mythical Mate*) on how coupleships go through stages. The first, the Romantic Stage, is all about bonding and connecting, as do a mother and infant. We bond around our similarities. The second stage, which we were now well into, is called Differentiation, and it's all about redefining oneself as a separate person inside of the pair bond, as does a toddler toddling off on her own. In this stage our differences become apparent and we need to develop skills for negotiating healthy balances between them.

The old model of relating that maintains we should suppress any part of ourselves that brings a partner discomfort ends up producing two half-people and is ineffective in bringing happiness in the long run. Pete and Ellyn's new paradigm was to celebrate and support one another's differences while simultaneously building new means of connection through negotiation skills.

Long story short: Yashi and I found that rather than hiding differences we could honor them and find ways to plant gardens for them. For example, Yashi loves to go off by herself on meditation retreats. Though I miss her, I support her doing something that fills her soul. As for me, much of the year I am out at least two evenings a week playing basketball or softball, which I love doing. Yashi misses me and supports me in doing so.

Not only do we thereby know ourselves better, we

support each other in being ourselves, thereby enriching our relationship.

We come to know ourselves better through more life experience, in and out of relationship. The better we know ourselves before we jump into relationship, however, the better our chances of going the distance.

If we know ourselves fairly well, we can readily disqualify a potential mismatch early on, before our hearts are too much entangled. The electronic dating services have raised the efficiency of this selection process by providing prospects with an extensive questionnaire that pinpoints such stumbling blocks as tobacco and alcohol usage, religious and political orientation, and even tastes in music. While I think that there must be a priority grid here, in that, for instance, I can accept someone with different musical tastes or even politics but not dishonesty, it seems to me that such a questionnaire can be a huge time and effort saver. If you are seeking a mate, know yourself well enough to be able to know and to state clearly the qualities that are important to you. If you know that you want someone who hates TV and is an ultra-fit athlete, or someone who can financially support himself and also wants children, hold out for that special someone who fits your qualifications. You will thereby increase your odds tremendously of going the distance and avoiding affairs.

Please notice that the assumption of such questionnaires is that people are answering them honestly. If you or your prospective partners are not, their usefulness is questionable.

Similarly, if we are in relationship and you are sneaking a cig every so often and telling me that you never do, I become confused and mistrustful when I smell and taste the tobacco on you. When the truth outs, as it always does over time, I am going to be less trusting of you in the future. Once I find that you have lied to me, I will never know for sure if you are telling me the truth about anything for a long time thereafter.

What to Tell Each Other

Obviously, we cannot share *everything*. My suggestion is to:

1. Say what your wish for.
2. Respond to whatever your partner asks directly about.
3. *Share whatever you are nervous about sharing.*

Of course you can drive a partner crazy if you make it a point, for instance, to say every time you feel a little flutter for someone who's attractive. The very funny film *I Am a Sex Addict* dramatizes this point well. I don't need to know about quickly passing fancies. However, if you persist in longing for contact with someone else and find yourself enjoying the secret, that's a particularly important feeling to share if you want to preserve your relationship. Similarly, if I am considering investing a large sum of money in a friend's enterprise, I need to make sure that you know about it and are in enthusiastic agreement.

If one day when I'm tired and grumpy I find I'm annoyed just being around you, I know that that's not about you. However, if I find that a particular action that you repeat is annoying me over a period of time, I can share that information so long as I don't make it about you:

"Geez, how come you keep bleaching your hair? It gets all straggly."

And instead make it about me:

"While I know how you do your hair is your business, I want to let you know that I really like it natural."

And of course I need to keep saying what I like:

"I sure like the way you kiss me hello."

Too many people will say what they *don't* like, so it comes out as a complaint:

"You never kiss me anymore when you come home."

Notice that the emphasis is then on how you not doing something annoys or upsets me and is therefore likely to trigger a fight. Much better to go for the wish:

"I'd love it if we could have a hug and a kiss when you come home."

Enough is enough

It is also important for each partner to be able to say when they have heard enough for that day. When I gave you the guideline in *Real Relationship* of asking for 100% of what you want, I didn't mean that you have to ask for it all today. Part of what most of us want is to simply relish being with a loved one, without feeling that we are always "on task" to meet the partner's needs. In that case, it's okay to ask for a temporary moratorium on wishes, truth, or talk. If you are truly "given out," that's important information for your partner. A loving partner knows she or he cannot get water from a dry well.

Additionally, when I can honestly say when I'm "given out," my partner can trust that it's okay for her to make requests when I am not saying that. She doesn't then fall into the trap of mind-reading: "I'm probably asking too much. He's going to get upset with all my wishes. So I'll shut up."

If you are thinking that, you can just ask me if that is the case. Do not presume that you know your partner better than he or she does. When I then say, "No, you're not asking too much. I really want to hear what you wish for," you can trust that I am telling you the truth.

Only a very few people ask for too much. Most of us aren't very good at asking and need to get better at it. But if your partner is asking more of you than you can comfortably give, you will need to say so. What you want to head toward is the situation in which you both ask for whatever you'd like and are also comfortable with knowing what your partner's limits to giving are. (We all have such limits.) When I know you'll ask for what you want, I don't have to be on constant alert trying to guess what that might be. When you know I'll tell you truthfully when I've reached a limit, you don't have to be eternally watchful that you're overstepping bounds.

Total transparency builds total trust.

Sharing Vulnerabilities

As we build trust in our relationship, we will be able to share our vulnerabilities, which are very hard for some people to share. The False Self likes to pretend that it is invulnerable and is embarrassed by what it sees as "weakness"—that it never lies, for example. The Real Self knows that, no matter how eternal we might be, it is extremely vulnerable in the embodied state. We can be hurt by a single word or even a look. We will abandon and let one another down in countless ways. We know that we are mortal and that our minds and bodies will ultimately lose efficiency and then disintegrate. We will all die. How do you feel about such facts of life and death?

As long as we identify with the False Self, we will be terrified of disintegration and death, for the False Self sees that as The End, which it is for the False Self. As we approach death all that is false begins to drop away. We realize that all of our achievements and wealth and status are now meaningless. This person who made these accomplishments, got that degree, wrote this book, achieved that golf score, owned that car, had those babies, is about to be no more. This body that served us so well until recently is now deteriorating and is perhaps racked with pain. The ability to think clearly is ebbing. All of who I thought I was is disappearing. As it disappears, what is left?

Many people who have "died" on the operating table and then been resuscitated tell a fascinating story. They speak of moving out of the body and into a sense of great peace. They find themselves surrounded by intense white light and feel a sense of blissful connection with the divine. When

they are resuscitated their first feeling is often one of disappointment that they have had to return to the embodied
state. Afterwards, they have no fear of death.[12] When you
approach death, you will have an opportunity to enter that
passage with vivid consciousness. But you needn't wait till
then. You can enter this state of inner peace and bliss right
now. How you can do so is the subject of a marvelous little
book by Eckhart Tolle called *The Power of Now*.[13] I recommend it to you highly. Many of his observations about relationships parallel my own. More importantly, he will lay out
a fast track into the Real Self.

You might take a moment to experience what happens
inside you when I bring up this discussion of final things.
Do you become uncomfortable? Frightened? Annoyed that
I would mention death in a book on relationship? Do not
judge your feeling response. Do your best to accept it with
compassion. Death is not a popular topic in our culture. In
fact, we do our best to hide it away from view.

Yet it is an ineluctable part of our life's journey, one of the
two certainties that Benjamin Franklin assured us of. When
you can open your relationship to speaking of such things
as death, you will find that you move into a much deeper

Exercise: Ask yourself this question: Is there anything
that I am hesitant to speak to my partner about? If so,
what am I afraid might happen? Can I imagine being able
to bring up anything with my partner? Even preparing
for our deaths? What does that feel like?

---

12   See Raymond Moody, *Life After Life* (1975).
13   New World Library, Novato, California, 1999.

level of connection than if you are only conferring about your favorite sitcom.

A possibility for your relationship is to have at least one person in the world with whom you can share anything. When that is the case, you form a bond with your partner that is irreplaceable. You have become best friends as well as best lovers. You have added another layer of protection around your relationship.

"(S)he Just Doesn't Understand Me"

These are, of course, the trite words that a new potential lover is most likely to hear from someone who's already in a relationship. The fact that they are often true is sad.

Pat and Dee had been together for fifteen years. A registered nurse, Dee had put Pat through law school. They were raising three incredible children together. Yet Pat found himself saying these words to a female partner in his firm. When he heard himself, he realized that something was very wrong and came into my office confused and conflicted.

"I'm a jerk," he said. "Dee has given so much to me. She was the breadwinner for three years while I went to law school and she's been the primary child-raiser while I've been getting my career off the ground. During these years it's true we haven't spent a lot of quality time together. We've both been so busy. Our main relating has been around raising our kids. And sex. We've always had a good sex life. We've been lucky that way. But we've just drifted apart. I'm not in love with her any more. And I have amazing feelings for Elizabeth. She really understands me. After all, she's a lawyer too."

I cannot tell you how often I've heard some permutation of this same story. I talked to Pat about the passing away of the Love Cocktail and how our feelings get lost when we're prioritizing career and raising children over feelingful time together. I suggested that he invite Dee to come in with him for the next session. He looked startled but agreed to do so.

When they came in together, Dee had the look of a deer in the headlights.

"What's this about?" she asked. "I thought we had a good relationship."

Clearly uncomfortable but forging bravely ahead, Pat affirmed that, while they did have a good relationship in many ways, he'd lost his loving feelings for her and was beginning to have strong feelings for a colleague.

Dee went white.

"What do you want?" she asked in a dangerously quiet tone.

"I want to get that loving feeling back with you," Pat said.

I asked Dee what she wanted. She burst into tears. Pat took her into his arms.

"I want to get that feeling back, too!" she sobbed. "It's been so long without it. I've been getting way too close to this doctor at work myself."

I want to pause this story at this point, although I'm sure you're eager to know how it came out. This was the break-through, however, because they were now being transparent and vulnerable with one another. I knew, at that moment, that they would be able to avoid the imminent affairs and get the loving feeling back in their relationship. It took them a few more sessions to be able to decide how to deal with the people they'd started to be attracted to and to find specific ways to rejuvenate their relationship. One of the most important means they found to revitalize their relationship was to co-create quality time together. In fact, they decided to have Dee's parents look after the grandkids for a week and went off to Tahiti on a second honeymoon.

I want to point out in passing that they had no problem with their sex life, which they both felt good about. Yes, sex is important but it is not the be-all and end-all of relating. Like Pat and Dee, you can be having good sex together and still not feel understood or loving. To cultivate that sense of understanding, couples must create time together in which they can be transparent.

Some Advantages of Being Transparent

When you are open and honest with your partner you have to be open and honest with yourself. Consequently, you get to know your Real, as opposed to your False, Self. Neuroscientists point out that we truly discover ourselves *in relation* to significant others through the activation of what are called *mirror neurons* in our brains. If you attempt to fake who you are, those neurons either don't activate or get confused—and we then get confused about who we really are. As Kurt Vonnegut put it succinctly, "Be careful who you pretend to be, because we tend to become who we pretend to be."

By committing yourself to honesty, you get to be loved for who you are, warts and all. You can then let down the tremendous effort it takes to fake it and relax into accepting yourself as you discover that your Real Self is actually loveable—which is difficult for many people to imagine might be true but is, nonetheless. You can then enter into a state of true tranquility. Imagine: Just being yourself and still being loved! Pretty sweet, eh?

Being forthright is also a lot easier than living a life of lies and having to remember which story you are presenting to which person. You thereby simplify your life and feel more relaxed and serene. As I like to put it, "Easy is right."

In addition honesty puts in place a powerful preventative against falling into an affair. If you are honestly reporting to your partner that you are beginning to feel strong feelings for someone else, the likelihood is that your partner will be highly motivated to address the issue before it gets out of hand. As will you, for you won't be able to kid yourself that it's no big deal. You catch it before it goes too far. You then have a chance to address what might be askew or missing in your relationship and thereby escape the agony of going through a break-up. Even if you are already in an affair, honesty (and a good therapist) can save the relationship 90% of the time.

Finally, you have the satisfaction of knowing that you are an authentic person who lives from a place of integrity. That is a knowledge more precious than gold.

I hope that I have persuaded you to consider moving toward the path of truthfulness. While it takes a bit of work to get there, I know that it is well worth the effort. I hope that you will be compassionate with both yourself and your partner as you become more transparent.

Oh yes, Pat and Dee. They are still happily together. After much soul-searching and discussion, they both decided to change jobs, a bold step in the middle of the Great Recession.

What it came down to was that they each knew that continuing in daily contact with someone that they were very attracted to was playing with fire. They prioritized their relationship above money and status considerations. This decision was probably a bit easier for Dee, whose occupation was in high demand in their community. She moved across town to another hospital. The commute is a bit longer for her.

Pat had to wrestle with the issue of leaving his prestigious firm and giving up a lucrative partnership. However, there had long been a part of him that wanted to scale down and practice on his own. Now he takes only those cases that truly interest him. He has more time to spend with Dee, and he tells me his tennis game has really improved.

They have a smaller income now, but a lot more time together.

"We have," Pat says with a broad smile, "managed to adjust. And our sex life is better than ever. When I think of how close we came to throwing it all away, I get the heebie-jeebies."

CHAPTER 3:
HAVE DELIGHTFUL SEX TOGETHER

*"When a marriage goes on the rocks,
the rocks are there, right there!"*
—Big Mama, *Cat on a Hot Tin Roof*

In Tennessee Williams' classic drama, Big Mama points to the bed to make her famous pronouncement. While that perspective is of course overly simplistic, a good ongoing sexual relationship is usually a powerfully bonding factor in relationship. In fact, a simple formula for relationship stability is:

*Frequency of lovemaking minus frequency
of quarrels.*

In plain language, couples who have more sex than fights tend to stay together.

When we occasionally experience the ecstasy that love-making can bring, we are lifted up out of our quotidian selves and touch the divine. That connection is very deep and reinforces our bonding. Though sex needn't always be cosmic. Just the simple pleasures of feeling skin-to-skin contact connects us, releasing surges of oxytocin into the bloodstream. Oxytocin, you will remember, is the bonding hormone.

Most of us are also aware that when the Love Cocktail is flooding our veins we tend to have plenty of good sex, but as that chemical booster rocket sputters, and we have to deal with midnight illnesses and who takes out the trash, we find ourselves making love less frequently and blissfully. As one of my students from the state of Georgia put it, "If you-all put a penny in a big ol' jar every time you-all make love the first year and then take a penny outa the jar every time you-all make love over the en-tire re-mainder of your relationship, you won't never empty that there jar." Whether that is true or not, this homely metaphor vividly clarifies the concept.

It also points up the fact that for most of us the lure of a new sexual relationship can be very tempting. When your old relationship has run out of Love Cocktail and a new one promises the excitement of that mixture of potent hormonal intoxicants, it's hardly a level playing field. How can we compensate for this unfair imbalance? We've already discussed how scrupulous honesty and meeting each other's needs can help. How can we apply these principles to our sex lives?

The fact is that maintaining a good long-term sex life, like any part of a good long-term relationship, takes consciousness and effort. You will need to be open and honest about what you like and don't like and able to share these facts about yourself with your partner in a kindly, non-judgmental manner. You will need to communicate and then negotiate. You will need to know about your partner's sexual needs and do your best to meet them. Ultimately, many couples find that their sex lives actually get better over time as they learn to communicate more openly. While many people complain about how boring a long-term sexual relationship can be, I would point out that finding ways to nurture sexual eroticism at home can be an act of defiance.

However, as with any part of our relationship, we can talk sex to death. By all means be directly honest about your sexual needs, but don't keep bringing up the same old same-old. I use a three strikes rule: I am willing to discuss what I want three times, asking my partner to reflect what she hears. But if she really doesn't want to go there, I'll drop it, carefully framing the drop. For instance, "I've requested that we maintain eye contact during orgasm and that's not happening, so I'm going to drop the request for now. If you find that you might be open to trying that again later, please bring it up."

Another obstacle that we all have to overcome is the sad fact that we have grown up in a culture that is itself quite conflicted about sex. On the one hand it is in our faces on billboards, in movies and magazines, in countless ads, and on the Net. On the other we are given the impression that there is something secret or dangerous about it, which we mustn't discuss openly. Most couples find it challenging to exchange basic information about their sexuality.

For instance, can you tell your partner something like, "I don't like my clitoris/penis touched directly until I am already excited. I get excited when you kiss me very softly and touch me gently"?

Or: "I love it when you suddenly kiss me hard and take me standing up with our clothes on."

If you are shy about divulging such information, or if you don't even know yourself well enough to do so, you have some delightful exploration ahead of you.

As did the adventurous middle-aged woman who was telling her girlfriends about how their couples' therapist had suggested that she and her husband might want to be open to having a spontaneous sexual encounter. They agreed to give it a try. She said her husband's eyes had met hers over an elegant, candle-lit dinner.

"With one hand he swept the tabletop clear of candles, plates and wineglasses, with the other he pulled me across it. He ripped off my panties and took me right there on the table. I had one orgasm after another. I was screaming my head off."

"Wow!" said one girlfiend, "That sounds awesome!"

"Well, I guess it was," sighed the woman, "but we can't go back to that restaurant anymore."

The Spectrum of Delightful Sex

I don't mean to suggest that sex need be "wowza!" sex to be wonderful. In Hemingway's *For Whom the Bell Tolls* the wise old woman Pilar says that the kind of lovemaking where the earth moves happens perhaps three times in a lifetime. Our culture programs us to expect earth-moving sex routinely, however. We don't see many Hollywood movies about 90-year olds or paraplegics playing happily in bed. ("The Sessions" is a delightful exception.) I don't know of a single song about the joys of cuddling. (I wish more creative artists would get on the stick!) There is a broad spectrum of pleasurable sexuality. Let's look at a few actual stories.

One couple liked to "hookup" when they woke up. After gently joining their genitals, they simply lay together, breathing in unison, without any movement. They would tell each other "Good morning" and that they loved each other. After about five minutes they'd gently separate to begin their day without either of them (usually) coming to orgasm.

An older couple, faced with his lack of erection and her thinning vaginal skin, would touch each other tenderly, using plenty of lubricant, and enjoy the sensations and their partner's excitation. Sometimes they orgasmed, sometimes not, but they both enjoyed their connection.

Another couple, one of whom is a paraplegic, continues to have an active sex life, though he has no feeling from his waist down. As usually happens in such situations, the areas just *above* that line have become eroticized, and he becomes quite excited by having his middle back or upper belly stimulated. He can still get an erection and orgasm, which she enjoys, though he experiences the orgasm throughout his upper body rather than his genitals.

"It was awful at first," he told me, "to lose the feeling in my genitals. That's what I was accustomed to. But as we experimented—and I have to give Sarah kudos for insisting that we do so, even when I was depressed and had given up—I found a whole new world of feeling opening up. It's been an amazing journey to a place that I would never have guessed was possible for me. And her."

As you see, there is a really broad spectrum of what lovers can find pleasure and delight in. Like Sarah and her husband, we need to have the willingness to experiment, to grieve what doesn't work the way you would like, and to discover what does. Our sexualities are powerful, if we but give them the chance.

What's It Take?

There is nothing quite so connecting for a couple as having enjoyable sex together. If you are having deeply and mutually satisfying sex with each other, much of the temptation of a new partner will be absent, although, as the story of Dee and Pat illustrates, sex alone is not a fool-proof cure for other issues.

What does it take to have delightful sex together? First, the wish to do so. Second, healthy bodies with balanced hormones. Third, knowledge of some basic sex techniques. Fourth, the ability to bring back the sense of mystery to our relating. Finally, and most importantly, the capacity to feel deeply and to express those feelings openly.

If you don't want to have sex with your partner, you will need to immediately address that issue. If you know why, say so. (It might be something as simple as bodily cleanliness. Unlike the French, most of us don't even know what a bidet is.) If you don't know why, get thee to a therapist and find out. Do **not** simply accept the fact and assume that your sex life, and your partner's, is over. If one partner, for whatever reason, isn't interested, the relationship will be at risk. If you don't share my love of playing softball, I can readily meet my need by playing with buddies. But what am I to do if you are no longer interested in sex with me when I am still eager? That is a dangerous situation that calls for medical or therapeutic intervention if the relationship is to be protected. For most Americans today sex is a normal and natural part of relationship. Don't deprive yourselves of it.

One common reason for a lack of interest in sex is hormonal imbalance or other health problems. When a couple comes to me with a sexual problem, I insist that they each get a complete physical from their primary care physicians. If there is a medical issue, such as low testosterone or a thyroid deficiency, that must be taken care of first. At the very least, we want to rule out the possibility of a medical issue. Many post-menopausal women find their interest in sex declining. Many older men find their erections flagging. Neither of these normal situations means that they need give up joyful sex together. Once we've taken care of the physical dimension, we can then move on either to increasing knowledge or to deeper feelings.

Knowledge

Let's start with the proviso that sex, like love, is a vast mystery about which we may never know everything. On the other hand, we do know quite a bit about sex that can be helpful to us. Most of us in this culture have inadequate or incorrect knowledge about sexuality. I remember well the day my loveable prep school biology teacher, Mr. Sanford, opened up the class discussion of reproduction by saying, "If you boys have any questions about human sexuality you want answered, I'm happy to do my best."

A hand shot up in the back of the class. I should say that at that time Andover was an all-male school and that Mr. Sanford was the only teacher who called us boys. We were, otherwise, uniformly called Andover *men*. I think this device was overrated as well as wholly inaccurate.

"What's the function of the clitoris during intercourse?" the owner of the hand asked.

Mr. Sanford scratched his white-haired head.

"I don't know," he confessed.

If a biology teacher at one of the top schools in the country didn't know such a basic fact, are you surprised that so many of us don't have adequate knowledge about so important a topic?

So the first thing I'd say is: Don't be embarrassed that you lack knowledge—most people are in the same boat. I've made a lifetime study (well, since I was eleven) of sex, reading everything I could get my hands on, taking classes and attending conferences, and I still discover something I didn't know every month.

My suggestion is that you, as a couple, educate yourselves together. Choose a book to read together[14] or explore on-line information.[15] Take a trip to your local bookstore and look through the sexuality section to find a book you both are drawn to. Let yourself be embarrassed when the hunk or babe at checkout tells you it's a great book. Enroll in a class with a teacher who's a bit more knowledgeable than was Mr. Sanford. Talk about what you're learning together, and experiment.

Let me hasten to add one word of caution. Don't become *overly* focused on technique. The key ingredient in good sexual connection is feeling, and if we are overly focused on techniques we can move out of deeper feelings. Dee and Pat could have taught a class on advanced sexual techniques, but when they misplaced their feelings for one another they were vulnerable to the attractions of a new partner. So, by all means get some basic knowledge that will help you know yourself and your partner better, but please understand that's just one narrow parameter of our sexuality.

---

14   I'd suggest beginning with Joannides and Gross, *The Guide to Getting It On* (2000) or Lonnie Barbach's *For Each Other: Sharing Sexual Intimacy* (1984).

15   I like the open frankness of <AskDanandJennifer.com>

Where might you start applying your knowledge? I suggest that you start with simple touching, which is a universal human need. Lacking it, babies die. So do relationships.

Touching

In order to begin you mutual exploration, start by discussing how you like to be touched in daily contact. Some people like a very gentle, teasing touch while others find that annoying and want a firmer one. Some people like to be slapped on the butt and others hate it. Most of us love to cuddle or kiss but at particular times and places. In fact, time and place probably change what kind of touch you are open to. Some people, for example, are shy about public displays of affection while others are more affectionate in public than at home. Find out what your partner likes.

What kinds of physical intimacy are important to you? When one popular syndicated column ran an informal survey, 8 out of 10 women responded that, if they had to choose between the two, they would rather give up sex than give up cuddling.[16] How important is cuddling to you? Do you ask for enough, in a non-demanding manner? Do you make "cuddling dates"?

What about love-making? Can you ask for that and make dates for that as well? And what about kisses hello and good-bye? Little touches in passing during the day?

---

16   A wise woman pointed out to me that, while she could have sex by herself, she couldn't cuddle by herself.

Cuddling Exercise: Make a date with your partner to meet at a certain time just to cuddle. Decide ahead of time whether you are more comfortable clothed or naked. Where will you do the cuddling—in bed, on the couch, in the hammock? For about how long?

Gently adjust your bodies together so you are both comfortable. You can spoon or be face-to-face or some other position. Try breathing in unison, then in counterpoint. Which do you like better? How do you feel with your eyes closed? Open? Can you gaze into one another's eyes? Or do you prefer not to?

If you wish, you might lie on your sides, face to face, and gently massage each other's backs. How does that feel to you?

Experiment.

Tell each other how this was for you.

By the way, do you remember the guideline from *Real Relationship* about five positives for every negative? Those positive strokes needn't be only verbal. Simply reaching out to touch your partner on the hand in a loving manner can be a big positive, as is a warm hug. Most of us love loving touch. If you are one of those who does not, be sure your partner understands that about you and find a mutually satisfying way to work around it.

A couple I worked with demonstrates this issue. Lila didn't like affectionate touch, except during sex. Jose had a big need for affection. (The gender stereotypes are often false.) They negotiated the simple solution of making love more often, but including extended foreplay, which made them both happy. She got more sex, he got more touching.

Exercise: Our early experiences of sex and touching are formative. What do you remember about the kinds of touching and displays of affection you experienced and witnessed as a child? Were you touched inappropriately? Spanked? Slapped? How did that affect you? How did you feel about your parents' displays of affection?

When I was a child, I felt humiliated by spankings—and I don't like being hit in any way today. When an early girlfriend liked to playfully punch my shoulder, I hated it. (Unfortunately, I hadn't yet learned to say what I liked and didn't like.) On the other hand, I loved it when my parents cuddled at the sink. Mom would be washing dishes and Dad would ease up behind her and embrace her from behind while her hands were in the soapy water. He'd also give her breasts a gentle, almost covert squeeze. Mom would giggle and say, "Paul, not in front of the children!" in a *very* loving voice. Every one of their four children loved being present for this connection. We could feel the love in the room as though it were a palpable substance, like warm cotton candy.

Of course, since we tend to repeat what we learned from our parents, I make a similar move with Yashi. But while Yashi likes that embrace, she doesn't like to be surprised by me grabbing her bottom when she's bent over looking in the fridge. We each need to get to know the specifics of our partner's preferences.

I have known many couples who became frustrated over such varying needs for touch. Each of them seemed to have a very different need in how it was to be manifested. You will need to say what *you* do and do not like and then negotiate a way that the touch will work for both of you. There is no "right" way to touch, or make love. One size doesn't fit all. You will need to explore what you like and don't like and communicate those likes/dislikes to your partner.

Remember to avoid you-statements that blame your partner, such as, "You should know better than to touch me there." Reframe them as information about yourself—and focus on the positive: "I really like it when you touch me here, in this manner."

The same is true for your sex life. Say what you *like*.

Are you at all surprised that I am talking about touch so much in a chapter on sex? Please understand that what we call foreplay goes on all day and all year. *It's everything that happens between you since the last time you had sex*. The more you express affection by touching one another in ways you both enjoy, the more you show one another kindness and consideration, the more open to other forms of love-making you will be.

Varieties of Desire

I have certainly heard people in couples' counseling say, "I'm just not interested in sex any more. If I were to do it for you I'd be violating myself." That is certainly a clear I-statement. What concerns me about this position is its remarkable lack of empathy for the partner. When I put myself imaginatively in the situation in which I'd lost my libido when my partner hadn't, I would be quite concerned about her and our relationship. I would check myself out physically with my doctor and then psychologically with a good therapist. I would ask to enter sex therapy. If all else failed, I would want to find a way that worked for both of us that met her sexual needs. If I had no interest in helping her meet those needs, I would suspect that I might be harboring resentment toward her.

I will routinely ask my clients about their sexual relationship. In my forty years of practice I have gotten an extremely wide variety of answers that match the wide variety of people in the world. Whatever people choose to do or not to do in the privacy of their own teepees is fine with me. As Shakespeare put it, "Let copulation thrive!" One couple told me that they were very happy with their sex life. When I asked them how often they had sex, they replied, simultaneously, "Once a year."

I must admit that I found that a tad surprising. But the important fact was that once a year was what worked for *both* of them. According to them, it met their needs.

In contrast, I recently read a newspaper account about a woman who, after a brain surgery, wanted to have sex twenty or thirty times a day. There was no way her husband could satisfy this need. She wanted to be free to have sex with whoever was available at the moment her desire struck. Her husband was understandably somewhat uncomfortable with that proposal. I wish I knew the rest of that story.

Recent polls suggest that young people in long-term relationship tend to have sex about once a week, though it's not uncommon for new couples to have sex more than once a day. Older couples, about once a month. There is no "right" frequency. It depends upon what truly works for both of you.

If you had your druthers, how often would have sex?

There are incompatibilities of desire. I have a male client who wants to have sex two or three times a day. The woman he's in love with might be interested, if all goes well, once or twice a month. You can imagine that kind of discrepancy might be a problem for them. But because they care, they're working on it: She's open to getting turned on more and he's learning what is likely to turn her on.

The range of human sexuality is wide and is probably mediated by deep structures in the brain. There are a few cases of radical incompatibility, such as the extreme libido in the case of the woman who'd had brain surgery. However, for most of us there will be some means of getting our needs met that we can accomplish with enthusiastic agreement. That is the important task of successful relationship.

Co-Creating Hot Monogamy

Steve and Donna came in because they were frustrated by what they termed their "incompatibility." Steve was a self-described "neatnik," while Donna saw herself as more "laid back." In their sex life, she wanted more spontaneity, whereas Steve needed a sense of safety and predictability. As happens in many coupleships, they had each become entrenched in one pole of the continuum. As we worked together, they saw that that wasn't the whole story: Steve really enjoyed some spontaneity, within limits, and Donna readily agreed that she didn't want to make love in the street. They needed help in learning to accept their differences and to negotiate a new option that worked for both of them. For instance, they could make a date for a specific time and place, which helped Steve feel safe, and then bring in something new. They really enjoyed my suggestion that Donna take one of Steve's old neckties and bind his hands behind his back, then take advantage of his helplessness.

Human beings seldom want only one half of any polarity, but wish to have some of each side, at different times. The poet William Blake called it the Doctrine of Contraries: For every need we have there is an equal and opposite contrary. For instance, we want *both* the thrill of excitement and the comfort of safety in our sexual lives. We love to have a deep, intimate, committed partnership with its sense of ease, comfort, and safety—and we love to have uncontrollable passionate lust. The challenge is how to find a dynamic balance between these powerful contraries.

The good news is that we can, to a certain extent, have both. The bad news is that we have to relinquish our addiction to being biochemically gaga. However, a prime pathway to getting a strong hit of the Love Cocktail from time to time is to have great sex together.

The challenge for those of us who opt for long-term relationship is to meet both our need for safety and our need for excitement. As with so many of our polarities, balance is all.

Let's think of this challenge historically. We fall in love with a virtual stranger who is his or her own person with a separate life. Uncertainty abounds. Will he call? Will she have sex with me? Is he disease free? A serial killer? Is there a future for us?

Passion is heading for its peak—both from the Love Cocktail and from the uncertainty. We like the passion but the uncertainty brings us anxiety. So we attempt to tame our mate and to make the relationship more predictable. We attempt to control our anxiety through commitments and plans and demands and pet names. We go to get our AID's test together. We negotiate monogamy. We work on our need for safety and predictability. One busy female client wished to write into her planner a half hour for sex during her frantic week.

And as we feel closer and less anxious, there is a golden period during which we seem to have a perfect balance between safety and passion. Everything seems to flow easily. We feel a lot of trust for our new partner but with the relationship being so unknown there is still much to discover and explore. Every day seems to bring a new and happier surprise.

And then, inevitably, there is that first disillusionment. It might be something small, such as when she keeps you waiting for fifteen minutes and you become anxious that she won't show. Or something bigger, as when you find out he's been dating someone else at the same time.

If we choose to go through the disillusionment together, we are then likely to redouble our efforts at creating yet more safety. He agrees to terminate the other relationship; she promises not to keep him waiting for more than five minutes.

As we construct greater and more enduring structures in our attempts to make love safe and secure, however, a strange thing happens: Over time, we feel less passion. We are now once-wild animals attempting to mate in captivity. As you may know, many animals in a zoo lose their capacity to mate.

There is an ironic paradox at the center of every long-term relationship: We want passionate sexuality and we want safety. But the sad truth is that once we "tame" our partner and he or she submits to our control, passion fades, because passion thrives on uncertainty, variety, spontaneity, and the unexpected.

The amount of passion in our relationships is directly proportional to how much uncertainty we can tolerate, within a safe and accepting environment.

A relationship without safety will soon shipwreck—or prove to be too anxiety-producing to sustain. A relationship without variety will tend to grow boring.

And so our challenge is to find the optimum balance between the need for safety and the need for variety.

Each coupleship will need to find a balance for this polarity in its own way. The couple who had sex once a year prioritized safety. Nearer the variety pole were Don and Mary, who'd been happily married, they told me, for going on thirty years. They had long ago gotten bored with what they called "vanilla sex." They liked the excitement of having sex in places where there was a threat that they might be interrupted—the back seat of their car, a bathroom at a big party, on an elevator, out in a field of flowers. They said that the unusualness of the setting and the slight danger of being discovered added spice to their sex life.

Do you find yourself judging them? What does that tell you about yourself? After all, they have enjoyed almost thirty years of sex with the same partner.

Balancing Safety and Variety

Exercise: How much safety, and of what kind, do you need? For instance, will you have sex only in a monogamous relationship with a partner who has passed medical tests proving him or her disease-free? Do you insist upon using birth control or not using it? What if your love-making produces a baby? Do you know how your partner will respond to parenthood? How will you? Do you want your partner to be gentle and tender or rough and forceful? Or both—at different times? Are you certain that he or she will be able to stop if you want to? Take a few minutes to list what parameters you need to feel safe. Which of these are up to you? To your partner? Are they specific and doable?

Once you have a list of what will help you feel safe in love-making, check in to observe how you are feeling. Are you comfortable with your list? Or does making it provoke some anxiety? Is there anything on your list that you are hesitant to discuss with your partner? Or does making such a list bring with it a sense of boredom? Can you observe your responses to the exercise without judgment but with curiosity?

After you've taken a few minutes with your feelings, you might be ready to move on to the contrary pole—variety. What variations, within the parameters of safety that you have created, would you like to experience?

Exercise: What kind of variety, when and where, would you like? Which other places might you enjoy having sex? The livingroom couch? A field of flowers? In what degree of dress or undress? What positions or practices would you like to experiment with? What are your fantasies? How might you play with them? Most importantly, what do you feel about all of this? Can you express those feelings to your partner openly?

Our feelings in and around sex necessarily pull us toward unpredictable variety. However much we attempt to make some portion of our lives totally safe—and one way we try to do that is to dampen down our feelings—we simply cannot shut them off completely for very long. They will erupt through even the most elaborate defenses, especially in sexual situations. Although some actors in the porn industry seem to be able to perform a sort of sexual connection with almost no real feeling, feelings have an amazing capacity to break through. I remember attending a live sex show in Denmark. The female participant shut her eyes and was clearly focusing on her own internal fantasies in order to act her part. The male did exactly the opposite—he kept stealing glances at the audience to keep himself aroused enough to perform. I realized that what turned him on wasn't so much the sexual act as the fact that an audience was watching him perform. Each actor was having feelings, though almost none of them were related to each other or the act they appeared to be participating in together: He had feelings about performing in front of strangers, she from her mental imagery.

Most of you reading this can remember a time when, during or after having sex, you felt an uprush of powerful emotion. Perhaps the earth moved. Maybe you felt a revulsion for your partner. Or found yourself suddenly weeping. Or laughing hysterically. My point is that feelings *will* erupt during sex. Rather than try to make sex "safe," I suggest that you go with your feelings and see them as an exciting and unpredictable adventure in your life. They will occur spontaneously. They are the essence of spontaneity.

"Spontaneity"

John came in frustrated with Karen that their sex life had evaporated. But whereas she wanted to set aside some time for erotic encounters that might include sex, he bristled at the concept of planning—he wanted their sexual connection to happen spontaneously, "like it did when we where dating."

Karen pointed out that when they were dating sex almost never occurred spontaneously: "Back then, we *always* scheduled our time together. I loved anticipating that we were going to be together on, say, Friday evening after work. I'd think about it all week. I'd decide what I was going to wear, consider what I wanted to talk with you about, and imagine how I'd seduce you. By the time our date came, I was frothing with pent-up desire that I'd been building up for days. So, yes, it didn't take much to get me going."

John thought about this for a minute or so, then nodded.

"You're right. I did the same. I'd walk into the restaurant stooped over so no one could see my erection."

After we all laughed at this image, I pointed out that while most of us love the idea of being swept away by passion, of being in the grip of something powerful, that such feelings seldom occur spontaneously. Generally, passion builds over time. Erica Jong's fantasy of the "zipless fuck" is just that—a delightful fantasy.[17] There are always zippers to negotiate, unless you're at a nudist colony. If spontaneous sex were going to occur in their relationship, it would already be happening and they wouldn't be in my office.

---

17   Jong, Erica, *Fear of Flying* (1994).

Like most couples, they would need to find ways to recreate the anticipatory excitement of their dating days. One ingredient of that was the fact that they had much more separate time then. Another was, as Karen had said, they had time to look forward to a planned date. Why not do the same now?

I pointed out that sex can never be planned—it always occurs spontaneously or not at all. What they could schedule was the *opportunity* for an erotic encounter. They could take the children over to the babysitter's, turn off their phones, and put a "Do Not Disturb" sign on their apartment door. They could put on romantic music or light candles. They could take off their clothing and feel the contact of their skin. But whether their bodies would then wish to move into sex was a mystery that they could not foretell.

Before they left my office, they made three dates for what they called EEs—erotic encounters—during the forthcoming week. Even John seemed excited about the possibilities.

At our "date" in my office the following week, they arrived a few minutes late and strolled in languidly, smiling happily.

"Well," John said, "you just accomplished a one-session cure."

Bring Back "Beginner's Mind"

What helps us to be open to the spontaneous nature of sex is to consciously cultivate "beginner's mind": A lovely practice from Zen to help us shed our preconceptions and to experience daily existence with more freshness.

We can bring back wildness into our seemingly safe

relationships by being mindful, on a daily basis, of the fragility and uncertainty of normal life. This will help us to resist taking our partners for granted and to see them each day with beginner's mind, as we did on that first day of falling in love when infinite potential lay before us like a yellow brick road.

Remind yourself that *all* relationship is uncertain: Either of us could be killed in a traffic accident today or by a heart attack tomorrow. When we part company in the morning, can we be sure that we will ever see one another again? Even our quotidian life is fraught with continual small abandonments: The withdrawal of love and affection when one or both of us is angry, the incapacity of illnesses, even the separate world of sleep.

Contrarily, when we suspend ourselves in the illusion that our relationship will be perfectly safe, given how enmeshed we have become, we lose our edge. By carefully deconstructing selected portions of our safety net, we also reinvigorate passion. The latest pop term for this process, "individuation," was lifted from the work of Carl Jung (who used it to apply to individuals) and is now being used to mean bringing into the relationship reminders of the reality that there are two separate people in it.

Charlie and Missy came in to see me in a strange state of blissful desperation. Almost two years in their relationship, they were pretty much joined at the hip like Siamese twins. They'd fallen in love "at first sight," according to Charlie, and had seldom been apart since the day they met on the job. They had breakfast together each morning, drove together to their company, where they worked in the same department, put in a hour of exercise at the gym after work, made dinner together (they were both vegans), watched the same TV shows, and went to bed at the same time. The only sense of space they had came from their decision to pretend, on the job, that they weren't really a couple. Their company had an unspoken rule forbidding employees from dating.

They said they were blissfully happy but also growing stale. I could almost hear their suppressed screams of quiet desperation. Although our societal fantasy is that such togetherness is ideal, in fact it isn't for most people. A disturbing research statistic is that the children of overly enmeshed twosomes are much more likely to be suicidal than those of parents who have a bit of space in their relationship.[18] When I suggested to Missy and Charlie that they might benefit from a bit more breathing room, their relief was palpable. Clearly, they had both sensed they needed space but neither had been able to ask for it. They needed an "authority" to legitimize it.

When I asked them how they could create some healthy space in their daily lives, they came up with several suggestions. Charlie loved to play golf but hadn't picked up a putter since he'd fallen for Missy. He was itching to get back out on the greens. He called his former golf buddies and set up a foursome for that Sunday afternoon. For her part, Missy wanted to get back to writing a book for children. She had just begun it when she met Charlie and had let it languish in a bottom desk drawer. She set up a writing schedule in the mornings, choosing to skip the commute with Charlie to work and have an hour or two a day to focus alone at

---

18 See, for instance, http://www.psychologytoday.com/blog/both-sides-the-couch/201201/untangling-the-bonds-enmeshment. I first heard this statistic in grad school and can't find the original study.

home on the book. They both liked the idea of arriving at work in different vehicles and at different times to thwart the budding rumors among their fellow workers that they were living together.

The next week when they arrived at my office, they were both glowing.

"It feels really good to get back out with the boys," Charlie said. "I didn't realize how much I was missing the camaraderie."

"I love getting back to my writing," Missy said. "And because we have the little breaks from each other our sex life has taken off again."

"Absolutely," Charlie confirmed, grinning from ear to ear.

Please understand that I am not saying separation by itself is good. I am talking about separation and individuation *within the context of togetherness—at least 15 hours per week of quality time together.* Some coupleships have too much togetherness and need to bring in some air; most coupleships do not share enough quality time. More about this in the chapter on time.

Consciously creating spaces between you in your lives is but one means of helping you to enter beginner's mind. Another is to break down your assumptions about who your partner is. Doing so is challenging, because our minds like to pigeonhole our realities neatly and become uneasy at having to shake up our perceptions. One part of us clings to a highly predictable world. Another relishes surprise and discovery. Here's one way to help you perceive your partner as if for the first time:

Beginner's Mind: Clear an afternoon. Make a lunch date at a new restaurant and arrive separately. Pretend that you are meeting for the first time. Introduce yourselves as if you were strangers. (You might even want to try on a new name.) How do you go about getting to know this stranger? Expect to feel some discomfort.

If you wish, one of you can invite the other home. As the "guest," see your dwelling and its surroundings as if for the first time. As the "host" how do you feel having this stranger coming home with you?

What happens next? Does one of you attempt to seduce the other? Verbally or non-verbally? Try a different way than the usual.

Imagine you are kissing this person for the first time... feeling this new body...seeing this new body...

What do you notice happening within yourself?

Sexual Feelings & Feelings That Come Up During Sex

In case you didn't hear me say it often enough in *Real Relationship*, feelings are the lifeblood of our relationships.

Those who repress their feelings tend to block their sexual feelings as well. Those who accept and enjoy their feelings can have a lot more pleasure during sex. Feelings are a powerful way to re-ignite passion in our long-term relationships. They are the ultimate aphrodisiac.

Exercise: Remember the last time you had sex. Were you able to be totally present, feeling what you were feeling? Or did you find yourself harboring a concern from the past ("She hurt my feelings the last time we had sex.") or worrying about the future ("I've got to make cupcakes for the PTA...")? Did you worry that you might be interrupted? That you weren't doing it "right"? Or that you might have forgotten to turn off the stove?

Could you allow yourself to breathe fully and noisily? Could you allow up the sounds that were inside you? Could you speak (or scream) your feelings? Could you be vulnerable with your feelings?

If you found yourself becoming distracted, could you ask for a break in the action? Could you accept that you were feeling something other than sexual passion? If you realized that an issue with your partner was intruding, could you ask to stop and clear it? Could you then return to where you'd left off?

By opening ourselves increasingly to our feelings, we increase passion in our relationship. Feelings are wild and unpredictable. The anxiety that attends them opens us to more passion. We have to be in our feelings to feel really sexy. Embrace your feelings rather than repress them. If you tell your partner when you are angry (using clear "I-ams") you will release blockages to your own sexual passion. As Shakespeare put it, "There is often a good night after a good fight." Remember, the fight must be a good, clean one based on genuine feeling and conducted fairly, without low blows. If you have any questions about what I mean by fighting fair, please review Chapter 12, "Constructive Conflict," in *Real Relationship*.

One of the primary ways that our sexual and loving feelings get blocked is by unspoken resentments, griefs, or fears. You might say to yourself, "Well, it's not a big deal that he forgot our anniversary," but then you find that you feel numb when he wants to make love. You might go ahead anyway and then find that you resent the fact that he orgasmed and went to sleep before you even got very turned on. When he starts snoring, you find you hate him and wonder how it would be with your boyfriend from high school. You can see the possibility for a huge downward spiral here.

If, on the other hand, you are able to say, "Before we try to make love, I have something I want to clear with you. I'm a little hurt and annoyed that you forgot that today is our anniversary."

Ideally, he'll be able to hear you compassionately and to respond, for example:

> "I can understand that you are hurt and angry that I forgot our anniversary. Thank you for clearing it with me. Is there an amend I could make for my forgetfulness?"

You might then be able to say:

> "Thank you for hearing me. Would you feel okay about giving me a twenty minute anniversary massage before we make love?"

Or whatever you think would work for you to remove the resentment.

Actually, the simple speaking of the resentment—and

the compassionate receiving of it—will remove most resentments.

As William Blake puts it succinctly:

> I was angry with my friend;
> I spoke my wrath; my wrath did end.

The same is true for hurt feelings or for fearful ones.

Jack, who was approaching 60, came in to see me because he was shunning sex with his wife, who was a ten years younger, because he was afraid "my dick will lie down on the job. Maybe I'm gettin' too old to cut the mustard anymore." He was increasing impotent and he had begun to avoid sex.

"I'm so focused on what's going on with John Thomas down there—or *not*—that I get tighter'n a drumhead inside."

I asked him what he was afraid of, besides not having a good erection.

"Well, that Betsy won't be satisfied and take up with some young stud," he confessed.

Had he talked to Betsy about this?

"Are you kidding? That's scary, man!"

I nodded and said, "Of course it's scary. Would you like to bring her in next time to have me help the conversation, or can you do it at home?"

He blew out a long breath.

"Let's role-play it a couple times," he suggested, and we did. He left feeling more confident that he could bring it up with Betsy.

When he came in the next week, he brought Betsy with him and seemed relaxed. Betsy wore a cowgirl's hat and boots and seemed entirely unpretentious.

"I brought up my limp dick with Betsy," Jack said, "and she said she didn't need a hardon to enjoy having sex with me. Can you believe that?"

I said that I could and asked Betsy if that was true for her.

"Yessir," she said. "I'm gettin' to the age when my skin's thinnin' out and it don't take long before a hard dick in me just hurts. But I do love all the other things Jack and me can do in bed. Just gettin' nekked and rollin' around together in the hay makes my day. I hated it when he was pullin' away from me, but neither of us could get it out in the open, for some reason. I wanted to come in and thank you myself for the help you give us. You saved our marriage."

She reached over and took Jack's hand, tears in her eyes.

I might have shed a few as well.

When Jack had been able to tell her what he was scared of, she had been able to tell him about her pain during prolonged intercourse. This vulnerability on their parts enabled them to release their ideas of the way sex "should" be and freed them up to enjoy it as it really was.

An unanticipated further benefit was that, relieved of the pressure to get an erection, Jack found that he sometimes got them, as often is the case. He could then wait until he was close to orgasm, then enter Betsy and climax relatively rapidly, before it became painful for her.

Show your vulnerability. Telling your partner how vulnerable you feel toward him or her will open you to deep passion. I think there is nothing so arousing for me as seeing my partner's emotional nakedness and her acknowledgement of how important I am to her.

The single most common block to happy sexuality is withheld feelings.

Avoiding and Dramatizing

We need to take a look at these characteristic tendencies in this context. Avoiders want to skip the feeling talk and get into sex, hoping that the resulting good feelings will wash away the bad ones. They will tend to be impatient with a partner's need to clear feelings, as in "Yeah, yeah, big deal. Can we have sex now?" That approach will of course only magnify their partner's discontent or fear. Avoiders will need to learn to enlarge their capacity to hear and deal with feelings.

On the other hand, Dramatizers, who tend to make mountains out of molehills, will feel the tiniest pebble under a stack of mattresses. (Do you remember the story of the Princess and the Pea?) What they can do to help the relationship is to continually process their own feelings away from the partner to move many of them down the river and to bring up for discussion only the ones that continue to bother them.

Of course Dramatizers and Avoiders tend to choose one another as partners with astonishing regularity. Here we find more evidence of the Doctrine of Contraries between, as well as within, people. The benefit of this arrangement can be that Avoiders necessarily become more compassionately aware of feelings, in others and in themselves, and that Dramatizers find themselves becoming more balanced. However, this positive process can occur only when each of them suspends judgment and understands their partner with compassionate tolerance.

Because both of them really want to achieve a positive sexual connection—and when they do they receive a big emotional pay-off—dealing with feelings around sex can be quite successful.

What happens if you thought the forgotten anniversary wouldn't bother you but you find that it does, when you're in the middle of sex? *Ask for a time-out.* There is no rule anywhere that once we're into sex we *must* continue. Sure, a time-out and feeling discussion will alter the mood—which is precisely the purpose. If your mood needs an adjustment, take a time-out to attempt to bring that about. Yes, your partner might feel temporarily annoyed that his pleasure is being interrupted. But he will hopefully understand that if it's not working for one of you it ultimately isn't working for both.

Please note how I am reframing *time-out* from the way it is customarily used—as a punishment for a child who is misbehaving (from the parental perspective). Actually, I am opposed to that practice by parents: Much better for a frustrated parent to call a *team* time-out, as we do in sports—a time for the whole team to take a breath, consult, and regroup. That's the way I mean it in this context as well: You and your partner are certainly a team in making sexual connection. If one of you is off, it will help to call a time-out and reset.

The very fact that your partner is willing to stop sexing and prioritize the team above his or her immediate needs communicates volumes. If one of you isn't happy with the way it's going, neither of you will be, ultimately.

Once you've had the clearing (see above), the one who requested the time-out can then say he feels good now and ask to re-start.

To add some feeling and fun to your sex life, I suggest the following simple and lovely exercise:

Exercise: Make a date to tell each other what turns you on. Prepare for the date by thinking about it, both remembering what you really like and imagining what you might like that you haven't tried yet. When you get together, flip a coin to decide who goes first. Give your partner specifics, such as, "I get really turned on when you wear a tux," "I get hot when you nibble the back of my neck," or "You drive me nuts when you gently and slowly lick me here (pointing)." As the Listener, use your Magic Mirror to be certain you've heard correctly. After ten minutes, switch.

At the end of the twenty minutes, tell one another how you feel inside your bodies.

"I'm Just Too Old for Sex"

That's what Jack—and many other older clients—have said to me over the years.

The myth is that as we age we'll lose our interest in sex or our ability to perform or both. The grain of truth in this archaic axiom is that our hormones *do* change and mitigate over our lifetimes. Women's change rapidly and radically at menopause. For some lucky women, sexual interest actually increases at this time, when they know they need not worry about menstruation or pregnancy. Some women actually find themselves with much more energy at this stage. Others experience the opposite, a diminution of sexual interest and energy, but can regain both with hormone replacement.[19] Women who have had hysterectomies are of course

---

19   See Louann Brizendine, *The Female Brain* (2006).

much more likely to need hormones. In self-report questionnaires, older women are more likely than men to admit they either have low sexual desire or no desire. They also say that they are more likely to lose desire for a long-term partner.[20] Men's testosterone levels diminish *gradually* from their highs in the 18-25 age range and some men's blood supply of the hormone can fall to low levels, for a man. (It is worth noting that men's levels of testosterone are nearly always 10-100 times those of women's.) For these men, increasing the testosterone level usually restimulates sexual interest. Most people can retain their capacity to be sexual for as long as they live.

The problem can often be physical, which is why I ask couples with sexual issues to have a complete physical exam. On the other hand, sometimes the issue is psychological and is perhaps best illustrated by the couple in their 60's I saw recently whose sex life had gotten lost. Let's call them Keith and Debbie. Though Keith was angry that they weren't having sex, he was trying to be understanding and accepting. "I ask if you're interested," he said, "and you always say no. I need you to desire me or I'm just not interested. I find my own desire diminishing, maybe from age and a long marriage, or maybe because I turn off to your rejections of me."

Debbie bristled.

"I have plenty of sexual juice," she retorted. "But it really turns me off when you try to make your disinterest about me. Don't make this about me. When we make a date and get naked together I get hot."

---

20 See, for instance, <www.mnn.com/lifestyle/arts-culture/stories/why-women-lose-interest-in-sex>

"Bull! We're naked in bed every night and you don't get hot!"

That was when I decided to intervene in their Blame Game.

"What's scary about sex for each of you?" I asked.

They both looked at me in astonishment. Until then, it hadn't occurred to either of them that they might be fearful underneath their frustration.

It turned out that Keith feared that Debbie didn't really desire him, which hurt him and made him angry. He was waiting for her to initiate sex, which she seldom did, which in his mind proved she didn't desire him.

Debbie needed Keith to initiate with her, to lovingly seduce her. Otherwise she wasn't particularly interested. But once he made a date with her and began caressing her, she would get right into it—and desire him as he wished.

Both of them were fearful of being the vulnerable one who said, by word or deed, "I really desire you right now." That block was preventing them from having any connection and contributing to a mutual resentment that further cooled their ardor.

I suggested that they set up a standing date so they wouldn't have to negotiate that step every time. They then knew that every Saturday afternoon at two they would take off their clothes and cuddle in bed, *without expectation*. I wanted them to be free from any performance anxiety. In fact, I told them that for their first date they were *not* to have sex. But they were bad and disobeyed me. They came in for their next session holding hands and giggling like teenagers and shamefacedly confessed that they hadn't been able to restrain themselves.

"Well," I said, "those who restrain their desires have desires weak enough to be retrained."

For some older folks with changing or diminishing hormones, the sexual drive may be weak. If neither partner truly wants other than cuddling, there is no problem. Usually, however, one partner will admit that he or she might like to give sex a try again. Once we know there is no physical impediment, and if their partner is willing, we can draw upon the power of the human mind.

Imagination

It has often been said that the brain is our most potent erogenous zone. Most of us have had sweet dreams that have led to orgasm. There are some women who can bring themselves to orgasm without any friction or movement, simply by fantasizing.[21] Most people have fantasized during sex. Yet many people believe that they should not fantasize during lovemaking. They tell me that it is a betrayal of their partner or that they should be able to enjoy sex and orgasm easily by being fully present.

Do you *should upon* yourself in this context?

In a parallel manner, many women believe they should be able to orgasm during intercourse with their partner. Yet the surveys prove, over and again, that two out of three women seldom or never orgasm with coitus alone. Most women, in fact, will need clitoral stimulation to be able to

---

21 "I'll Have What She's Thinking," William J. Broad, *The New York Times* "Sunday Review" (29 September 2013).

orgasm. But if they deny this fact and insist that only the coital orgasm is "real" or "mature" (as did Freud, who also admitted he didn't understand women) they are going to be frustrated and unhappy.

By the way, I hope that all you women reading this book know that *every* woman who wants to can orgasm.[22]

 Do not deprive yourself of this delicious experience.

In the same way that a woman can put pressure on herself that she should orgasm coitally, anyone can "should" upon themselves to never fantasize during sex. But why deprive yourself of the kind of pleasure clitoral stimulation or fantasy can bring you? With our sexuality, as in so many parts of life, one size doesn't fit all. There is no "right" way to do it. Find out what works best for you. If you like it, why deprive yourself? It's certainly not fattening.

Marisa could orgasm quite readily multiple times by fantasizing but not at all without doing so. She felt she was deficient and "should" be able to orgasm just by feeling her love for Carl when they had sex. She couldn't. She could either be present with Carl, in a warm and friendly sort of way, or she could get into her fantasies and become a Sex Goddess. (Which mode do you think that Carl preferred?) Because she was a feminist she judged herself harshly that her fantasies often had a masochistic element—for instance, a common theme was being ravished by several men who seemed bored with the job.

There is a difference, we must all remember, between our fantasies and reality. Later in her life, Marisa was actually

---

22 See Lonnie Barbach, *For Yourself: The Fulfillment of Female Sexuality* (1976).

raped. Nothing about that reality was erotic. What she felt was terror and repulsion.

People are, as you are aware, different. Marisa had a marvelous imagination. What purpose would it serve for her to deprive herself of the pleasure it gave her, and Carl? If someone enjoys their fantasies, however strange those fantasies might seem—and some of them are really creative[23]—who are we to sit in judgment? Instead, why not accept them, in the same way that most women will need to accept the need for direct clitoral stimulation?

Marisa herself was quite articulate about the alternate perspective. As she put it: "I feel bad that I have two different sides. I can be here and now with Carl, and enjoy that, or I can do what I call 'go away' into my mental imagery and orgasm. I feel like I'm betraying him with my fantasy partners. I wish I could just orgasm looking into his eyes."

As to the objections of "betrayal" or "not being present," that is an individual preference. If you feel uncomfortable with the more creative fantasies, you can actually use fantasy about your *partner* to bring you even more present. For instance, I can imagine the lovely pink folds inside of my partner's vagina as I slide deep inside her. She can imagine my penis swelling and purpling as it does so. We are totally in the now, with this particular person. We have simply added the dimension of the imagination.

Once you are comfortable (and excited!) imagining the present more vividly, you might wish to experiment with the past. Because Yashi and I didn't know each other as virgins,

---

23   See Nancy Friday, *My Secret Garden: Women's Sexual Fantasies* (1974).

I thought it would be fun to go back in time to that point through the power of the imagination. We both entered the delightful fantasy of being sixteen again and began exploring each other's bodies as we might have done at that age. Yowza! Who says it's ever too late to have a happy childhood?

Even if you did know each other at sixteen, you can return to that mindset and re-enter that time and place imaginatively.

What Marisa and Carl came to be comfortable with was using her fantasies to bring her to the threshold of orgasm and then becoming totally present with Carl as she reached orgasmic inevitablity. She would open her eyes and look directly into his as her body bucked and shook. She had to learn to accept herself as she was. Carl had no problem with that. In fact, Carl felt that he was the luckiest man in the world.

"The Eyes Are the Mirrors of the Soul"

Cicero noted this important fact centuries ago. You can use it to your advantage in your relationship to continually reconnect with your partner and retrigger doses of the Love Cocktail. All you need to do is to set aside a few minutes of uninterrupted time to lie down facing each other and gaze into one another's eyes.

Exercise: Turn off the phones, tell the kids you're going to have some adult time, and lock the door. Lie down on the bed on your sides facing one another. Look directly into your lover's eyes. Breathe deeply and fully and don't speak.

At first you might feel embarrassed or uneasy. Acknowledge the feeling and let it be. Then bring yourself back to your lover's eyes. Look deeply into them. Are you remembering to breathe deeply? Good. Observe how you are feeling within—and enjoy each part of it.

A Few Ideas to Try

I'll bet you found that this simple exercise triggered feelings for you. Our eyes provide soulful contact. We avoid contact by not looking into each other's eyes—or wearing darkened glasses. I have often helped couples reconnect simply by insisting that they maintain eye contact.

I learned this intervention from the children at the day care center I worked with while I was earning my graduate degree in clinical counseling. I had the seemingly preposterous idea that I could teach these children, between three and five years old, negotiation skills. My supervisor was skeptical, believing them too young to grasp the concepts. I agreed—about the concepts—for these were children whose brains were of a developmental level not yet ready for much abstract thinking, which usually comes at about twelve years, when the corpus collosum is fully mylenized and can readily connect the right and left hemispheres of the brain. However, I believed these youngsters had the ability to be present and honest in a way that few adults did.

So when Zachary grabbed the doll Katie was playing with and Katie screamed at him, I didn't penalize either one. I confiscated the doll temporarily and asked Katie and Zach to sit down facing one another to work out their problem of how to share the doll. At first, neither would look at the other and they remained intransigent, but as soon as I got them to look into each other's eyes, they melted.

> Zach (beginning to tear up): I'm sorry I grabbed your doll. I just wanted to be the dad.

> Katie (putting her arm around him): You can be the dad. Just don't grab our baby. That hurts her feelings.

After many such interactions, I became convinced of the power of eye contact. I also convinced my supervisor—and the entire group of skeptical supervisees—that young children could negotiate better than most diplomats when I played my recordings of them doing so.

The recent discovery of the workings of our mirror neurons provides a scientific explanation for what I discovered intuitively—and which most of us know anyway: When we look deeply into someone's eyes we will tend to feel loving.

Touch Power

In the above example you will notice that Katie put her arm around Zach to comfort him. Most of us know how wonderful it feels to be touched with consciousness. When I began working as a therapist, I knew that I'd need to take care of myself so I could be present for my clients. To that end, I committed myself to making sure I had both my own therapy session and a massage every week (among other things). Mind and body care. I have continued to follow this practice for going on forty years. I relish my weekly massage, when I can surrender to caring, conscious touch that absolutely rejuvenates me.

Being touched is a fundamental human need, yet many people attempt to do without it. Even those in relationships. Many children experienced injury around unloving touch and shun it later in life. If you are one of these people, I encourage you to reclaim your birthright of loving touch by releasing that pain of childhood through feeling-based therapy. You deserve the full humanity of the joy of touching and being touched every day.

At the beginning of a relationship, the potent power of the Love Cocktail can override many people's ambivalence about touch and bring them into close, intimate contact. Picture, if you will, two lovers entwined on a park bench in Paris in the springtime. But as time passes, many couples I know find that they're fortunate to touch once a week. Simultaneously, they find that they have more "issues" in their relationships.

Often they attempt to repair the estrangement by talking about it—sometimes interminably, to the point of mutual exhaustion. When they come in to see me in this state, I will often point out to them that, while our culture has an unreasonable faith in reason and the power of the word, both reason and verbalization have definite limits. I suggest to them the following exercise, which I pass on to you:

Exercise: First, stop trying to solve issues by talking about them. Give yourselves a "speech fast." Express your caring for each other through gentle, considerate touching. Give your partner a hug in the morning when you first wake up. Touch her hand at the breakfast table. Rub his neck while he's washing the dishes. Cuddle on the couch to watch a favorite program together.

Take turns asking for some skin-to-skin cuddling. Try spooning. Then face-to-face, without and then with eye contact. Synchronize your breathing. How do you feel? What do you notice?

Try this exercise daily for a week and then talk about what you have discovered. Yes, there is a place for verbal communication. Remember to focus upon what you are discovering about *yourself*. Don't criticize your partner. Most of us are especially vulnerable to sexual criticism.

Some Other Things to Try

Seek variety within the safety of your relationship. Share your fantasies and play with them. Here are a couple examples to get you thinking of your own:

- Become a 16-year old virgin. See your partner's body as if you've never seen the opposite sex before. Touch tentatively. Let yourself be fearful and awkward. Pay close attention to how you actually feel.

- One woman, who liked being seduced, would hand her husband a book of matches before she left for work. The matchbook had the address and telephone number of a bar on the cover. Inside the matchbook was a time, such as "6 p.m." At that hour he'd enter the bar, take a seat next to her, and try to pick her up as if she were a stranger. She'd pretend she didn't know him and attempt to brush him off. "Get lost. I'm married." He'd have to be persistent. "O.k., so you're married. I'm married, too. Could it hurt if we talked a little?"

- Do you have a dark fantasy that you'd be ashamed to tell anyone about? Of course you do! Make yourself vulnerable enough to share it with your partner. Is there some way you'd both be comfortable playing it out in a safe way?

- Buy one of the books that will give you some ideas, such as Laura Corn's *101Nights of GRRREAT Sex* (2000) or Alex Comfort's *The Joy of Sex* (1972).

Remember that the only rule you need follow in your sex life is that you are both in enthusiastic agreement about what you do together. What other people might think of you is none of your business. In fact, there is usually a boosting of excitement when we consciously break taboos. It can be a lot of fun to be a bad girl or bad boy and to do what Mommy told you never to do. Whatever you decide to do together, discuss it and make agreements that provide you with the requisite safety that you need. Then go for it. You can always take a time-out or stop if you become uncomfortable. Agree on a bail-out phrase (such as "Mayday!") that works for both of you. I suggest you not use "No," however. "No" can be a real turn on for some people. Why do you think that might be?

A Final Word

Delightful sex is enjoyable in itself while serving as a powerful bonding agent in any relationship. As a formerly Puritan culture, we tend to view something that is so pleasurable with a jaundiced eye and try to rationalize it as a necessary evil to produce children. One hopes that we are emerging from that cultural darkness.

If you can educate yourselves about sex, talk about it together as a couple, and enjoy sharing your feelings and your imaginations, you will build a powerful bond that is unlikely to be threatened by outside attractions.

I wish you much joy together.

CHAPTER 4:
TIME TOGETHER, TIME APART

Had we but world enough and time,
This coyness, lady, were no crime.

...

The grave's a fine and quiet place,
But none, I think, do there embrace.
—Andrew Marvell

As Marvell's wonderful poem points out, we have scant time together to enjoy each other, even during a lifetime. As in Pat and Dee's relationship, the daily priorities of life—training for and developing a career, making enough money to live on, paying taxes, raising children, and having a few minutes here and there to enjoy some solitude or time with friends—seem to suck up all the available time. When Pat and Dee were first courting, they squeezed their time mercilessly to find a few extra minutes to be together. Pat told a story of how Dee would come over to the law school library, where he had a work-study job ten hours a week, and help him return books to the shelves just so they could have a few minutes to chat and maybe steal a kiss in the stacks. They both laughed fondly at the memory.

But when Pat first joined the firm, the unspoken expectation was that the young lawyers would put in 80 hours a week if they wanted to be made partner—and they both wanted him to make partner with the much larger remuneration and perks that status would bring. So they rationalized that they'd have to deal with the grind for a couple years to get what they wanted—a secured position for Pat and lots of money for both of them. But by the time Pat made partner Dee had babies to raise. She was fortunate to have a position that gave her six months of maternity leave. When she went back to work, she arranged for a three day week and a nanny, but she was incredibly busy with their children on her "off" days and the Monday-Wednesday-Friday eight-hour days often stretched to ten as she caught up on paperwork.

She hardly "had a minute to breathe," as she put it, but she did take a half-hour lunch break in the hospital cafeteria. There she met a young doctor who really appreciated her knowledge of the hospital's politics and procedures. He kept showing up when she lunched, ostensibly to draw on her fund of knowledge, which she found quite flattering. Though her experience was that most doctors treated nurses like second-class citizens, she felt like a respected human being with Sam. She noticed that she had begun looking forward to their chats and was somewhat disappointed when he missed a day or two.

But then he showed up at her desk when she was doing her paperwork after hours and she found that it was more interesting to talk with Sam than to fill out all the damn forms. She could take them home and do them while she watched the kids or while Pat was relaxing in front of the TV.

"Jeez," Pat said to her one night, "they sure mire you down with paper at that hospital."

"It's awful," Dee said, not looking up—and feeling just a little guilty. What scared her was that she *liked* feeling guilty. It gave her a rush. There was now a part of her life that was just her own.

When they had sex that night, she let herself fantasize that it was Sam in her arms.

"Wow!" Pat said. "That was better than ever."

A minute later, he was snoring like a sawmill while Pat watched storylines take shape on the darkened ceiling.

Most people lead very busy lives. If we can share a good-bye kiss and have a few minutes to make love at night, what more should we expect? We know we love each other—shouldn't that be enough?

In a word, No. Love is not enough.

If we are to have successful long-term relationships, we need to pay careful attention to time management, for time together and time apart. Both are crucial for healthy relating. In this area, as in most, one size doesn't fit all. I know couples who actually enjoy spending months at a time separated by half a globe and others who shun the briefest lack of contact. You will need to decide together what balance works best for both of you.

The Time-Management Grid

Unless you are a lawyer billing clients in six-minute intervals, you probably have never filled out a time-management grid. The purpose of doing so is to see fairly precisely how you actually spend your time. Be prepared to make some surprising discoveries, even by simply recording hourly how you spend your time.

Take an 8.5 x 11 piece of blank paper, place it before you sideways, and, using a ruler and a sharp pencil, mark off 18 or 20 horizontal lines. Next, mark off 8 vertical lines.

In the far left-hand column write down the hours, beginning when you awake and ending when you go to sleep. (If
you get fewer than 8 hours of sleep, you'll need additional
horizontal lines.) Across the top put in the days, Sunday
through Saturday, leaving the first upper left square blank.
(Confused? See Appendix A for a prototype.)

Carry this grid with you for a week, filling in each hour
of the day with how you spent the major portion of your
time that hour, starting with, for instance:

> 7 a.m. Dream Sharing/ Shower/Dress/Breakfast
> 8 a.m. Write
> 10 a.m. See first client

Continue entering your daily activities, hour by hour
(and wonder how those attorneys do it every six minutes).

When you've completed each day, review the column
that evening and make any additions that you need to make.

At the end of the week, total up how many hours of your
life that week you spent:

1. Intimately with your partner.
2. Doing activities that nurture you.
3. With your children.
4. With friends.
5. Working.
6. Doing household chores and maintenance.
7. Watching TV, being online, etc.
8. Sleeping.
9. Wasting time.

What do you learn? Are you shocked by how little time you are allocating to what you would tell me is most important in your life? And by how much you allot to stuff you don't even like to do? What do you need to do about that?

Are you getting enough sleep? Most Americans don't.

How we spend our time is how we live our real life. How do you want to live yours?

Exercise: (This works best if you have a friend read it to you or record it and then listen.)

Darken the room and lie down comfortably. Close your eyes and follow your breathing. Imagine that you have just found out that you will die within the year. How do you feel, knowing that? Take some time with these difficult feelings.

Now think ahead: How are you going to spend your remaining time? What would you like to do that you haven't done, or that you'd like to do a lot more? What's on your Bucket List?

How much will you work, if at all? If you are going to work, what would you change about how you do it?

Who do you want to spend time with, if anyone? What would you like to do with them? What do you want to know about them that you haven't found out yet?

Do you have any unfinished business with anyone that you would like to clear up before you die? Is there anyone you haven't told you love that you'd like to say that to, before you go? Or how much you appreciate them?

What is the very first thing that you feel is most important that you do right now, while you're still alive?

Take a few minutes to write down what you've discovered.

This is a challenging exercise for most people because we avoid thinking about death in our culture. Consequently, we tend to live carelessly, as if we had infinite time on our hands. We don't. One thing I can tell you with absolute certainty is that one day that old one whom we call Death will reach out and tap you on the shoulder.

The Yaqui shaman Don Juan suggests that we use Death as our advisor.[24] Our death, he says, always walks beside us, a step behind our left shoulder. Our death is with us from the day we are born. When you are considering a choice or a course of action, turn to your left and consult your death. For instance, I can work on this book this morning or play my computer game. When I turn to my left and ask, "Mr. Death, which of these choices do you advise me to make?" I feel a chill. It's important to me that I complete this book before I die, and I know that moment could come to me, or any of us, at any time. That gives me a unique perspective.

Similarly, when I actually faced death (twelve years ago, with a diagnosis of melanoma in a small mole on my back), I was filled with a host of feelings, terror and grief principal among them, which I had to process daily for several weeks. Then my mind became incredibly lucid and I could look at my life as if I were seeing it through a reversed telescope. (I was reminded of Dr. Samuel Johnson saying, "Nothing clarifies the mind quite so much as knowing one will be hanged in the morning.") I was somewhat surprised to find that I was delighted with almost all aspects of my life—my wife, my children, my friends, my work, my play, my home. The

---

24 In the novels of Carlos Castaneda. See, e.g., *The Teachings of Don Juan: A Yaqui Way of Knowledge* (1968).

one corner of it that I found repugnant—having to work with insurers as a "preferred" provider—I immediately dispatched. It was as if I'd taken a fifty pound weight off my back. In the face of the reality of possibly dying in a short time, the choice was easy.

What issue in your life might you wish to consult Mr. Death about?

What would he say about the time you put into your relationship?

Time Together

When I tell couples that they need to be spending *at least* fifteen (15) hours a week together, they often look at me as if I had just asked them to rebuild the Twin Towers *and* a new mosque. The main objections are two. The first and more common is:

> "There's no way we'll be able to find fifteen hours
> in *our* week! We barely have time to sleep as it is!"

I point out that if one of them were to begin an affair, he or she would have little trouble finding fifteen hours per week to spend with the new lover. In fact, you have a choice: Spend fifteen hours a week with your partner or anticipate that one or both of you could begin to spend that time with someone else.

I perfectly understand how what we need to do to sustain existence sponges up all our available time. In fact, sociologists have come up with a fascinating precept:

*Work expands exponentially to fill the
available time.*

When we prioritize work and other activities over relationship, we will in fact discover there is no time left for relating.

So we must reverse the prioritization, placing our relationship higher in importance than our work or a fascination with technology. Yes, you will then have 15 hours less per week to work, surf the social media, play computer games, dust the car, or rearrange the knickknacks. But you will then work smarter, not longer, and get what needs to be done more efficiently.

Furthermore, you'll find you have created the time to fall back into love.

Take it a step at a time. Start small. In *Real Relationship* I suggest that you begin by taking *ten minutes* at the end of the day—right after work or when the kids are in bed—to reconnect. Do so by creating a "sacred space"—turn off the phones and tell the kids and other relatives that Mom and Dad are going to have some Special Time and are not to be interrupted unless the house is on fire. Flip a coin to decide who'll go first. The winner has five minutes to speak about his or her state of soul at that moment. The Listener just listens, silently, *looking into the Speaker's eyes*. Eye contact between you is very important. After five minutes, change roles.

Do this for one week and you will be amazed by how differently you feel toward one another, with the expenditure of one hour per week.

The second objection, however, is that one or both

partners are terrified of the idea of spending so much time together.

"What will we *do*?" they ask. "Can we watch TV?"

Exercise: What did you do when you were first falling in love and couldn't wait to be together? Did you make love a lot more than you do now? Did you have long talks about what you hoped for in relationship and life? Did you want to know everything you could about your partner? Did you play together, go dancing, take long walks or bike rides, or escape for weekends at a quiet B & B on the beach? What else? Give yourself plenty of time to revisit those thrilling days of yesteryear.

Okay, how many of those activities would you like to reinstate in your relationship now? How are you going to create the time? The most important togetherness you can apportion is some alone time when you can be meeting each other's primary needs. Yashi and I call this One True Love (OTL) time.

OTL Time

Yashi says that the concept of OTL time is one of my two great original contributions to the institution of relationship. The idea is quite simple—together, as a couple, you set aside an *inviolable* block of time that recurs on the same day at the same time every week to meet a few of each other's primary needs.

I have primary needs for good sexual connection and

affection, Yashi for affection and conversation. Both of us like to play together. To meet these needs *at least* on a weekly basis, we set aside four hours of time every Wednesday to be alone together in the middle of the day. This time is sacrosanct. If a client needs an emergency session, she'll have to wait. When a good friend or relative comes to town, we tell them we're tied up until after 3 p.m. Only in extremes do we negotiate a substitute time for our date and that quite infrequently—only once in the last year, for example.

So what do we *do?*

A Typical OTL Date

Today's a typical OTL date: We're going to meet up on the "Ditch," the canal that carries water down from the mountains, to hike along the broad pathway bordering it, beneath tall firs and pines. Since today is "her day," meaning she gets to set the agenda, which we alternate doing, she will be the first Speaker. On the way out for the mile or mile and a half, she will get to talk about anything, though we usually focus upon a transparent State of the Soul revelation. I'll hear how she is doing physically, emotionally, mentally, and spiritually, four vectors that we have found enlightening over the years. She might share a dream with me. She might have something to clear with me. My job is to Listen and, when she requests it, to reflect. If she wants my input on something, she'll ask for it. Otherwise, I follow the guidelines in the chapter on Listening in *Real Relationship.*

At the turnaround point, we will switch roles: I will talk, she will listen. Same rules.

We practice transparency and let our partner know how we really are. We get to have a good listener really attend to us. We clear any junk that might have come up in our relating.

We also get some good exercise and some breathtaking views of the beautiful forested valley that embraces Nevada City like a white gem in a green ring, while having the sweet songs of the running water and the multitude of birds as background music. Our walk-talk takes an hour or so.

Next, we'll go out to lunch together, so OTL has come, inadvertently, to have a double meaning. Today we're going to have a fajita salad on the deck of a favorite creekside restaurant, so we'll continue the running water theme. Over lunch we'll continue sharing, but with a more back-and-forth style.

Finally, we'll come home, take a shower together, and get into bed. Usually we make some very sweet love together, have a bit of a nap cuddling, and then another shower.

If neither of us must run off to work, as is usually the case, we'll extend our time together with a cup of coffee while we read the papers, sharing comments on the articles we find compelling.

I often work for two or three hours after OTL time—these clients probably get the best Belden of the week. Meanwhile, Yashi usually prepares dinner Wednesday evenings. I like it that way because, for some reason that you can probably intuit, she makes especially fabulous meals on Wednesday evenings.

After one of her fabulous meals, we'll usually read aloud to one another or watch a DVD together. We don't count these "extras" of the wonderful dinner together or the cuddling while watching *The Princess Bride* or *Casablanca* as part of OTL time itself, but they do tend to be permeated with the good feelings that follow from that date. They are a sweet bonus. When we watch a TV program or a DVD, we make frequent use of the pause button on the remote, so we can exchange thoughts and feelings about what we are watching.

If you're counting carefully, you'll notice that we're approaching half of our weekly 15 hours in a single day.

Special Time Together

I suggest that you consult with one another and create such a day for yourselves. Come up with your own name for it: "OTL Day" is already copyrighted. Together, specify a certain time frame on one day a week (the same time on the same day is best) that you designate as Sacred Time for your relationship. Do the Listening Exercise for one hour—30 minutes each way. The most important agenda item is to clear away any misunderstandings or hurt feelings that might have been withheld during the week. Then you can negotiate wishes.

At the beginning of our relationship, when we had more problems to solve, we budgeted a 50-minute hour each way. Adapt this time frame to what works for you. However, I strongly caution you to not to go past fifty minutes. Classes and therapy sessions are limited to that number for a reason—research psychologists tell us it's the upper limit of the human attention span.

There are many advantages to having a set time each

week to do this. First, you don't have to take the time and effort to negotiate it over and again. Second, you're more likely to keep a date that you know is coming at the same time on the same day each week. Third, you know you will have a chance to clear something at that time. You are therefore less likely to blurt something out before you've given it processing time—which blurting is likely to lead to long and painful drama. Fourth, if, by the time you get to your day the issue has become irrelevant, you don't need to waste time on it.

So that's the agenda for the first hour or two. What about the rest of the time?

Do something fun together. Reward yourselves for having done the hard work of clearing and communicating. Make love. Go out to lunch. Take a swim in the river. The idea is to make your Special Time fun and pleasant as well as challenging. By linking the fun with the hard work, you condition your mind to see the work as not so hard—and to actually look forward to your Special Time.

Special Time will make a world of difference for your relationship. You will have to work at getting it in place at first. Do not allow anything to usurp that time.

If you must miss it, negotiate a "make-up" session. For instance, Yashi just spent eight days in silent meditation at Spirit Rock. On the day before she left, we made sure we had Special Time, as we did the evening she returned. What I am saying is to prioritize your relationship above all else. Keep your date together through all the vicissitudes of life. If you absolutely must re-arrange, do so only as a last resort.

What you are then metacommunicating to each other is "You and our relationship are more important to me than anything—other than my relationship with The Great Mystery/God." You are saying it with deeds, not just words.

These two practices of daily and weekly time alone together will meet many of your needs for connection, conversation, and recreation. If you also make love on that day, you also meet needs for sexual fulfillment and affection. Make sure you are *both* getting at least one need met every time.

Creating Other Time Together

Once again, look to your top two or three needs. How will you each get yours met? As I mentioned before, many couples set up a Date Night when they can be alone together to talk, face to face. Once our eldest child was a year old, Gail and I had a lovely young woman named Mary Jane who came every Friday night while we went out for dinner or a movie and some time to talk uninterruptedly. Mary Jane was an important part of our family for many years.

Although we had a family bed, which meant that our children were welcome to sleep with us if they chose, we never experienced it as an interference with our sex life. If we wanted to make love at night, we'd leave the bed and go elsewhere. During the day, we'd tell the children we were going to make love and not to interrupt us unless there was an emergency. They never did. And they learned that parents do have a sex life.

One objective I've focused on in my own life has been to find ways to minimize the amount of time I spend doing minimally meaningful work, such as sweeping the deck or struggling with insurance companies to meet their obligations, and maximizing the time I have with my loved ones. Think about it for a minute: Most of us spend most of our precious time doing meaningless tasks, many of which aren't even necessary. Simone de Beauvoir pointed out that much "work" involves washing dishes that will just become dirty again, dusting shelves that will be dusty again ten minutes later, or cutting grass that will just grow tall in a week.[25] This kind of work is like treading water, efforting just to keep afloat. It can be discouraging, especially in contrast to the more productive labor of building a house or raising a child.

I remember well the day I was busy washing dishes and my children were tugging on my trousers asking me to play with them. I started to say something like, "Lads, can't you see that I'm busy setting you an example of how to be a non-sexist man?" but then it hit me like a thunderbolt: While there would always be dishes to wash, I had only a few precious years in which to play with my sons.

The same, as I hope is obvious, is true for our relationship with our partners. What matters more, that you make time to make love or that you chat on Facebook? You might wish to take stock of your own situation and ask yourself whether you are spending the most time with what matters most to you. Where we put our time is a valid measure of what's truly important to us, no matter how we rationalize otherwise. If you are actually spending it at work or watching TV or rebuilding the '55 Chevy, then that's what's most important to you.

Therefore, we can readily judge what's most important to us by how much time we are willing to invest in it. I spend

---

25   *The Second Sex* (1953).

about 30 hours a week with Yashi and about 30 hours a week working. I spend over 80 hours a week with myself, which is the most important relationship for me to attend to.

Time Apart

Did I shock you with that last little stat? Excellent! I wanted to keep you awake this late in the book. The stat is true, though you'll probably accuse me of cheating when I point out that I get an average of eight hours of sleep a night, which is already 56 hours of "alone" time every week. But even if we overlook that kind of statistical fudging, I budget about 30 hours a week for myself—and I do it first, before I put in time for anything else.

If you've ever flown on an airplane, you know that the flight attendants instruct you that, in case oxygen is needed and the little yellow masks drop down from overhead, you are to put on your own mask *first* before attending to your children or those around you in need of assistance. In this case, *selfishness is the most effective policy—as the first step.* Once you have assured that you're getting plenty of oxygen, *then* you are in position to help others.

The same is true in relationship. When we fail to prioritize meeting our core needs and try to meet everyone else's, we will end up burnt out and resentful. To change the metaphor, you can't get water from a well gone dry. When our wells give out, so do we, and we become the kind of people even we don't want to be around. On the other hand, when make time to take care of ourselves, we are able to be kind and considerate and caring.

What do you need to do to keep your own inner well filling up and spilling over with cool, sweet water?

You will need time for yourself.

Sleep is an excellent example. Most of us don't get enough sleep—and we tend to suffer from that deprivation and to become grouchy partners. Any of us is able to be more loving and giving when we are well rested than when we are sleep-deprived. Sleep is also crucial to our overall health. Set aside sufficient time to get a good night's sleep—or pay the price of being a grump who has frequent illnesses. I almost never use an alarm, but allow myself to sleep until I awaken on my own. When I had babies who awoke in the night, I got up to comfort them and would then nap with them during the day to make up the difference. Be creative—but meet this primary need.

Similarly, you know you need to eat moderately of nutritious foods several times a day and get aerobic exercise for at least half an hour a day. This is not rocket science. These factors are, however, fundamental to our overall well-being and mood. A long time ago, Plato counseled us to create "a healthy mind in a healthy body." His wisdom is still pertinent today.

You will also need time to be with yourself, in solitude. Introverts will need more solitude than extroverts. Some people, runners for instance, will find ways to meet a couple of needs simultaneously—exercise and solitude.

I know that to fill up my own well I *must* have the following on a daily basis:

8-9 hours of sleep
1-2 hours of exercise

1-2 hours outside (can combine with exercise)

2+ hours of writing time (in solitude)

You can count that I need a *minimum* of 12 hours of time for myself per day. If I short myself on any of these requirements for more than a day or two, I start getting as cranky as I do if I'm overly hungry.

I also get an hour-and-a-half massage each week and observe my weekly "Soul Day" religiously (as described in Chapter 3).

Exercise: What do you need to give yourself on a daily basis to replenish the sweet water in your well? Weekly? Monthly? Yearly?

Many people find it important to take twenty minutes each morning and evening to meditate. There are many benefits from such a practice, including lowered blood pressure. I like to greet Father Sun in the morning and express gratitude for being alive another day, and then take a few minutes to watch the sunset and to review the good parts of my day by asking myself, "What do I feel really good about having done today?"

These are examples of daily rituals to help us become more conscious. You might also want to schedule a yearly one. For example, Yashi and I take two weeks every August in the High Sierra to backpack, the first of which is time just for us. The second week is our Contacting Mother Earth workshop that includes a Vision Quest. During the two-day Quest portion of Contacting Mother Earth, each of us has one full day and night to be off alone while the other stays in base camp in case one of the Questors needs assistance. This is an annual renewal and spiritual pilgrimage for us. I didn't fully realize how important it was for me until I missed it one year to attend my mother's funeral in Ireland. That whole year I was "off" a little, as if I were living an inch or two from my body. Up in the mountains the next year I wept with the joy of feeling my body and spirit soaking up what it had been missing.

What do you need to do on a regular basis to renew yourself physically, emotionally, mentally, and spiritually?

Fill in Your Time *First*

On Sundays we sit down together with our calendars to plan our week. Before that meeting each of us has already blocked out time for ourselves. We don't make late-night plans because we know how important our sleep is to us. I set aside each morning from 8 to 10 for writing, in solitude. I also set aside an hour or two for exercise—softball, basketball, gym time, hiking, etc.

When you mark your calendar for your own time first, you are honoring the importance of it—to you and to the relationship. You are making sure your oxygen mask is in place first. Note that your own time does *not* include work time. Only after we've written in our own time first do we move on to the next priority—relationship time. Work time comes *after* that, in third place.

Too many people fill in their own time *last*, if at all. I know people who give up precious hours of sleep to carve out a bit of time after the family has gone to sleep or before anyone wakes up. And they often tell me they feel guilty about taking *any* time for themselves.

Feel through the guilt and be Selfish. That word is thrown at us from early in childhood in an attempt to control us—and is still used by other people to do so. While it may be quite effective in turning us into other people's servants, it is an absurd and illogical guilt trip. As you feel through the guilt you will probably uncover a great pile of resentment at how you have been manipulated by this single word.

Though I don't often agree with Ayn Rand, she has brilliantly skewered this guilt trip in a nifty little book she wrote with Nathaniel Brandon titled *The Virtue of Selfishness*.[26] The authors point out that selfishness, the powerful drive to protect ourselves and get what we need, is universal to all life. It is a given. But our Judeo-Christian heritage, in the attempt to counterbalance it with selflessness, has overtilted us in the opposite direction, that of self-sacrifice, exemplified by Jesus' death on the cross. We have become consumed with an ethic of sacrifice, which denies our basic instincts.

Once more we see an example of Blake's Doctrine of Contraries, in which neither side is totally effective by itself: Selfishness v. Selflessness. As humans we have a need to express *both*. We need, selfishly, to put on our own oxygen mask first, *then* to attend to the needs of others. It's a two step process. If we leave either out, we are only half human.

The Selfish part of you knows that you need time and space for yourself, to do those activities that you love that nurture you. You *must* sleep, eat, breathe, play, do meaningful work, accrue knowledge, love others and connect with

---

26   1961

them. These are not options but necessities in human life.

The Selfless part of you knows that you gain a great deal from serving others: By raising happy children, building a satisfying relationship, making the world a better place for all of us to live in, and assisting those in need or ill-health.

The question is: How do you strike a healthy balance between these two important parts of yourself? What I can tell you is that if you only acknowledge one side of the polarity you will fall out of balance and be ineffective.

In my own life I have had to learn to take care of myself first, which was a difficult learning at times. By doing so I have also been able to be a good father to six children/step-children and to hundreds of other children I have coached and taught, from pre-school through college. I have also been able to be an effective therapist for hundreds of my clients. One of the most important things I have been able to pass on to these children and clients is how they need not be hapless victims but active agents in their own lives, by being appropriately Selfish as well as Selfless.

Plan Relationship Time

I love Dr. Willard Harley for coming up with his very specific and unequivocal rule: You need to spend *at least* fifteen (15) hours a week of intimate time with your partner. And not just in being in the same ecosystem—but in consciously meeting each others' needs. Too many couples occupy the same physical space while seldom actually connecting. Plan at least fifteen hours each week in which you are *connecting*: With face-to-face intimacy, including love-making; with intimate conversation; with affectionate talk and touch; in playing and laughing together; in working on a common task—and doing those things that each of you really enjoys. How might you begin? I'll give you a few ideas by sharing with you some of the things Yashi and I do together.

The most important date we reaffirm is OTL time. Because it's always at the same time on the same day, it's a no-brainer that takes no effort to negotiate.

> *I strongly suggest that you find ways to limit the number of negotiations you have to make so you can use your negotiation energy on the most important ones.*

Next, we pick a Date Night, often Saturday. What do you like to do on a date? (What did you do when you were courting?) Do you both like to dance or attend a concert? Picnic at the beach on a blanket under the stars? Or simply hang the "Please Do Not Disturb" sign up on the door? What is *fun* for you both? You don't need to spend money to have a fun date.

Next, we each sign up to cook dinner for three nights at a specific time, on one of which we cook together. Cooking together is one way many couples like to share time. (In contrast, on Soul Day we have a "bum night," making our own dinner from leftovers.) We usually go out to eat together on the seventh day. We have now planned for six dinners together when we'll be able to eat a good meal and converse in a leisurely manner. Simultaneously, we co-create a shopping list. (We take turns shopping, on a weekly basis.)

Simply making plans together is something we find

enjoyable. Part of happiness is being able to look forward to pleasurable times that you know are upcoming.

Our after-dinner time is flexible, unless we specify otherwise. Usually, we decide how we feel over dinner—and often end up reading aloud to one another or watching a movie on DVD while cuddling on the couch. When we get snowed in and the electrical lines go down, we break out our games and play "Ticket to Ride" or "Quiddler" in front of the fire. Occasionally, we'll go out to enjoy a play or to meet friends to listen to some good music.

Unless we plan them otherwise, weekends are similarly flexible. We will usually spend an hour or two doing the laundry and cleaning the house and a couple hours attending to the land—planting the garden, repairing the sprinklers, culling the weeds from the pond, cutting down dead trees and splitting wood for the winter. I like to make frequent use of the hammock that overlooks the pond, for my cloud studies.

On Sundays Yashi likes to have a leisurely brunch together—and then we might exercise our option to jump back into bed. Then I'll fetch the paper and we'll read it together over a cuppa. In the afternoon, we'll call our children and family members and then perhaps take a hike in the mountains or a swim in the river. On other weekends, such as the one coming up in San Diego, we'll get together with some of our children or good friends.

While we both believe friendships are an important part of our lives, they come at a lower priority than our own relationship or those with our children. Some couples do almost everything with friends. By all means, nurture your important friendships. Just don't prioritize friends over your partner to the point that you dilute your primary relationship.

Don't forget, while you're planning your week, to put in time for your children, if any. Put that in right after relationship time. Special Time with your children is precious. When my children were growing up, I made sure that I had a few hours alone with each of them each week to go to the zoo or the Exploratorium, to take a hike or kick around the soccer ball.

I hope that you get the picture that, planned or unplanned, it is important to invest a lot of time in your relationship. The most important thing is to make some *firm dates* each week that both of you can look forward to. I give you our examples not to say that you should do it the same way but to simply give you one model. If you are much younger than we and are raising children, you'll be budgeting more time with them and the PTA and soccer practice. I spent a couple hours in my children's classrooms every week through elementary school and coached their teams three days a week in three seasons (soccer, basketball, and baseball) for sixteen years.

In all fairness, I should confess that since my first child was born, I have worked only half time. I owe this breakthrough to Gail, who already had two children but was happy to have two more with me—if I would agree to be 60% Mr. Mom. I was more than happy to do so. I had a challenging conversation with my then-boss, who finally agreed to cut my hours in half, and I was then free to take on the lion's share of the child care. I got to have an intimacy with my children that few fathers experience. I loved it, and at times I found it hard work. I cannot imagine how one parent can be a full-time caregiver. I can also say that it was the most rewarding experience of my life.

At the same time, I discovered that I really *liked* working half time at my chosen profession of psychotherapist. I looked forward to my work as a pleasant balance with my child-raising duties. I could be fresh and present with each client during a four hour day. When my children went off to school, I decided not to add hours of work to my day because I felt the balance was right for me and that I would continue to love my work if I didn't overdo it. I therefore had the time to coach my children and work in their classrooms.

In grad school I'd done a lot of reading in cross-cultural anthropology and found, to my utter shock, that the average amount of time so-called "primitives" devote to work is between three and four hours per day. *What?!* Don't we have the advantage of "labor-saving devices?" How can it be that they work a twenty hour week and we in "advanced civilization" work at least twice that?

Why this strange fact has come to pass is an interesting discussion beyond the purview of this book, but you might wish to speculate about it a bit. I'll give you a few hints to prompt you: Agriculture, the Industrial Revolution, and sugar.

The point is this: For millions of years of human history we have worked a four hour day. Rather suddenly, we started putting in much longer hours with very few days off. The Biblical injunction that we should rest on one day a week was then a benison. Only when we unionized did we trim our work week back to the standard 40 hour week, which seemed much better than what had come before. However, we're still way out of our natural comfort zone.

What do you want to do about that? I want to plant the seed to inspire you to work less and enjoy play and your relationships more.

Most of you will probably want to schedule more time to get together with friends or go to parties or the opera or line dancing than we do. Just be sure to schedule your personal and relationship time first. That is what is most important but seldom urgent. Don't let the unimportant emergencies of life dictate how you budget your time. Effective bosses are very good at creating emergencies that require you to work extra hours.

Now Put in Work Time

Your calendar is probably at least half full at this point. Good! *You're prioritizing what's important over what's merely urgent or necessary.* Too many of us, for too much of our time, do what's urgent rather than what's important. And much of what we believe is necessary, isn't.[27] Now fill in your work hours. I understand that most of you reading this book will say, "I have to be at work no later than nine and have to stay till five, if I want to keep my job." That's the tyranny of the traditional 40-hour week and most employers are happy that their employees buy into that as the "way it should be."

If you're working more than 40 hours a week, please take a hard look at your priorities. We can thank the labor

---

27 You might want to take a look at Stephen Covey"'s book *First Things First* (1994) for a thorough discussion of the differences between what's important to you and what's merely urgent or necessary and how to reprioritize your time and manage it more effectively.

unions for the 40-hour work week—don't undermine their sacrifice in bringing it about (good people died to do so) by allowing yourself to be exploited by your employer. Even if that employer is yourself.

Would you be happier working fewer and/or more flexible hours? Might your boss be open to restructuring your working time? Do you get nervous just imagining talking to him or her about that possibility? What does that tell you?

Are you one of those people who much prefer to work than to relate to your spouse and family? Is everybody happy with this arrangement? Are you sure?

If you're restraining yourself to 40 or fewer hours of work per week, you'll have time for yourself and your relationships—partner, children, family, friends.

If you're one of those unfortunate souls whose boss insists upon rigid rather than flex-time hours, your task might be more challenging, but please at least *ask* the taskmaster whether there might be a bit of flex in the work hours. Very few bosses today still insist upon nine to five. They realize that such rigidity fosters resistance and that if they accommodate their workers those workers will get more work done in less time.

You say you love your work? Great, I do too. And what I shoot for is to get done in four or five hours what a drudge will accomplish in eight or nine. I do that quite successfully. Remember that *work expands exponentially to fill the time available*—and sharply limit the time available for work. You'll discover that you'll work much more efficiently. Don't work long, work smart.

One of my clients is a successful home builder who used to put in 80 hour weeks before he consulted with me. He's made a few changes. Now, his way of working smart is to get up at 5:30 a.m. to do his paperwork—paying the bills, making out bids and so forth while eating a good breakfast his wife makes them—and then making his calls at seven. By half past he's out on one of his jobs, making sure everyone's there and troubleshooting any hitches that have come up. He then makes his rounds to the other jobs.

He meets his wife for a lunch date at a restaurant at noon, then plays a round of golf with buddies before picking his kids up from school at 2:30. He has some good time with the kids and then makes dinner along with them for the whole family. Sometimes he has an additional call or two to make while chopping the onions. When his wife returns from her job a little after five, they sit down to eat dinner together, watch a little TV, and put the children to bed so they can have an hour for themselves before they turn in at 9:30.

On any given day, he has a couple of one-on-one hours with his wife, a couple with his children, and an hour and a half for himself. He manages to run a big construction company working about six hours per day, 30 hours per week. His weekends are free for family time—and more golf. Saturday night is Date Night and Sunday morning is OTL time.

He tells me, "I like the sense of order and balance in my life now. And I've cut my work time more than in half without sacrificing quality or income."

"Balance is All"

Shakespeare said that long before I did. It's a good rule of life, right up there with "All things in moderation, including moderation." If we are spending most of our time working or arguing with our partners or befriending Facebook or whatever, we lack the essential balance that leads to the good life. As multi-dimensional beings, we need to feed and care for each of our proclivities.

One of those is our primary relationship. Another is our relationship with ourselves. All too often, we will put these most important relationships on the back burner and expect them to take care of themselves. We cannot do so without paying a tremendous price. As I hope this chapter has persuaded you, we must create and nurture time for ourselves and time for our primary relationships if we wish them to thrive.

The Greeks, who came up with a number of good ideas, such as the shape and size of the Earth, democracy, and the Pythagorean Theorem, put it this way: You must have awareness of *all* of the gods. If you only worship Aphrodite or Hera you will be out of balance. Aphrodite will help you fall in love, but takes off for Santorini when the child is born. Hera is the one who will help you with the childbirth and household management but who isn't very good at the arts of love. In modern psychological terms, if you are only interested in erotic love, you will suffer. If you are only interested in childbearing and the household, you will suffer. If you overfocus on work or the rational, you will suffer. You need to balance, with moderation, these different arenas in order to live the good life.

Once you have constructed such a life for yourself and your relationship, you will value it highly—and be quite reluctant to jeopardize it. While it will probably take you some time and effort to build such a schedule, and to reprioritize time for yourself and your relationship, keep tinkering until you construct a workable system that gives you at least fifteen hours a week together and a commensurate number of hours for yourself. Consciously keep filling the two wells—that of your own soul and that of your relationship—with cool, sweet water. Then notice how your life deepens and enriches.

Another way of filling yourself and enriching your relationship is to have a lot of fun together, which we turn to in the next chapter. Fun thrives on spontaneity and the unpredictable. Part of how we balance our relationships is, after building in some safe predictability, as we have in this chapter, to then bring in fun, spontaneity, play and laughter to avoid getting too serious or stuck in a rut.

It's the Doctrine of Contraries once again: Safety and predictability on the one hand, spontaneity and surprise on the other.

Balance is all.

CHAPTER 5:
PLAY AND LAUGHTER IN RELATIONSHIP

He who laughs, lasts.

There's an old Mary Lawton cartoon showing a zombie-like couple sitting at a table with martinis in front of them, staring grimly past one another and looking as if they had just eaten bad oysters. Above them are the words "THE RELATIONSHIP WAS GETTING SERIOUS." Although I was unable to track Mary down to obtain her permission to show you this frightening image, believe me when I say that it is truly terrifying as well as hilarious.

Answer the following questions True or False:

1. I am in a serious relationship.
2. I am serious about my relationship.
3. My partner and I are quite serious about each other.

If, as almost anyone does, you answered one or more of these questions "True," your relationship is probably not playful enough. Given a cultural norm that we are either frivolously uncommitted (as in "playing the field") or serious, most of us will choose to be serious. Yet the very qualities of seriousness that we bring to our relationships tend to stifle loving feelings.

The great poet Chaucer said:
Love will not constrained be,
But leaps high walls to be free.

Being too serious is a misguided attempt to build high walls of predictability around love, which only prompts it to leap outside them.

Love begins in freedom and uncertainty, compassion and acceptance, magic and bliss. We feel ourselves expand and become better than we are. We leap high walls with a single bound, sometimes literally, as both Romeo or Tristan do. Marvelous synchronicities occur.

I remember how Yashi and I brought each other the same kind of rose and the identical poem to our first date. That kind of magic is a little eerie.

And, as we have discussed, because we want to keep these feelings around in the future, we begin to clutch and hold on like baby monkeys to their mother's fur. We become less playful and more serious.

Love thrives on fun and play and spontaneity and the unexpected as well as safety. When we try to fence it in too narrowly with predictability and promises, seriousness and expectations, it tends to leap those walls and run off down the street looking for something new.

We have already examined several antidotes to this problem, including finding ways to get our core needs met, being honest and open with each other, having delightful sex together, and creating time together and time apart. Along the way, I have mentioned some reminders about such basic considerations as cultivating a beginner's mind to prevent us from ever taking our partners for granted, manifesting radical acceptance so we allow our partners to be free, speaking with kindness, and being at least as respectful of them as we are of our friends—important concepts covered more fully in *Real Relationship*. To this growing list we now turn to how to bring more play and laughter into our relationship.

How Can We Avoid the *Serious Rut*?

We need to use our creativity to balance our human tendency to want to put everything into predictable order. One way we can do that is to find ways to bring a little bit of change into our safe and predictable lives.[28] To give you an idea of how simply you can do so, try this exercise:

Exercise: (You'll need a partner for this). Stand facing each other and study each other for one minute—look at your partner's hair, face, clothing, shoes, jewelry. Now turn your backs so neither of you can see the other and take another minute to *change six things about your appearance*. Turn your glasses upside down, rumple your hair, unbutton your blouse, take off one shoe, and so forth. Use your imagination. On the count of three, turn back to face each other at the same time and look at each other. Identify six things your partner changed. Do this before reading any further.

Did you laugh when you saw your partner's changes? We tend to laugh at the *unexpected*, the changes in the predictable pattern, at what is "silly." Laughter and play keep upsetting the applecart of predictability—and help us see one

---

28   Some people's relationships are overbalanced toward the unpredictable pole; they'll need to bring more safety in. Others are overbalanced toward the serious pole; they'll need this chapter. Which are you?

another anew. They prevent hardening of the attitudes—and, as recent research shows, of the arteries. An ancient Chinese saying puts it neatly: "Every laugh adds one day to your life." Modern research confirms that laughter oxygenates the blood, relaxes the body, plumps up the thymus gland, and increases the efficiency of the immune system. Norman Cousins healed himself of a deadly disease by laughing at Marx brothers' films, and went on to contribute to research at UCLA into this connection between laughter, joy, and healing.[29] Most importantly for our chapter today, a healthy dose of laughter will shake up our tendency toward overseriousness and help us actually have fun together.

Malik and LaVonne

Malik and LaVonne were a handsome young couple who came to my office ready to throw in the towel on their relationship.

"It's just not much fun anymore," Malik said. LaVonne agreed with a slow nod of her head. Both looked glum.

They had met at a famous West Coast university, where they fell in love, getting married on graduation. They had dedicated themselves to making sure that minorities weren't excluded from the voting booth, a worthy cause about which they were both passionate. They agreed, further, that the cause had become their life and that their relationship had fallen back to a distant second place.

When I discussed the importance of time together, they readily agreed to make the effort, but then reported back that it just wasn't *fun*.

---

29   *Anatomy of an Illness* (1979).

"All we do is talk about our freakin' job," LaVonne said.

I pointed out that they were in a serious rut and had them do the prior exercise. They exploded with laughter and gave each other a big hug.

"That's the most fun we've had since we stole the Axe!" Malik said, referring to an incident from their college days. LaVonne agreed. I prescribed more play and laughter in their lives, including many of the suggestions in this chapter.

Laughter In Relationship

Why don't we laugh more, once we get past our addiction to seriousness? I think there are at least three primary reasons:

- We wait for something to be funny.
- We're afraid someone might laugh at us.
- We're afraid of hurting someone's feelings.

We'll examine each of these blocks in turn.

The first laughter-blocker—that we should wait for something to be funny—is a misconception. We don't laugh because something is intrinsically funny—*things are funny because we laugh.* I think William James was the first one to point out this cogent truth. Don't take my word for it. Try it out yourself:

Exercise: Go "Ha-ha!" if that's too challenging, try "tee-hee." Good. Again. And again. Keep it up. Experiment. Maybe "hee-hee!" or "haw-haw!" or even "ho-ho!" is more your style. Laugh harder. See what happens.

Laughter is a physiological mechanism of the body, not unlike sobbing, taking place largely in the diaphragm. All you need to do is to begin laughing and pretty soon you'll think whatever's happening is funny.

You don't need a reason to laugh. Laughter is a-logical. In fact, asking "What's so funny?" is a sure laughter-killer. Don't ask why. Just do it and enjoy it.

Exercise: Need prompting? Get a laugh tape. Listen and laugh along with it. Almost all sit-coms use a laugh tape. Or you can try <laughteryoga.org>

As you laugh more, life and relationships won't seem so serious. They may even seem funny. Laughing will make you happy. There it is, folks, at no extra charge, the Secret of Happiness:

The secret of happiness is—to laugh.

Two Exercises to Do Together: Spend five minutes a day every day this week laughing with your partner. How does it change the way you feel about each other?

Also: Share embarrassing moments. They're a rich source of laughter. Tell each other about your first date, the time you laughed so hard you wet your pants, the day you forgot that zipper. Laughter relieves embarrassment, or any painful feeling, and turns it into joy.

These exercises will get you started laughing together. Become a laughter-hunter. Find all manner of funny media, from films such as *Airplane* or *A Fish Called Wanda*, to Swami

Beyondananda's hilarious recordings. Read funny books aloud to each other. Right now we are reading Mark Twain's *Autobiography*, which is more fun than most of what's on Comedy Central. Seek any opportunity to laugh *with* (as opposed to *at*) people. Laughter is contagious. It also joins people.

A woman I know will walk up to perfect strangers who are laughing and join in. When she's had a good laugh, she'll thank them and go about her business. No one has ever had a problem with her doing this. People who are laughing are open for company.

Laughter is a way in to love. Don't wait for it. Go for it.

A "Sense of Humor"

When researchers study happy relationships they ask, "What enabled you to be together happily for so long?" The two most common answers are:

1. We accept one another as we are.
2. We have a good sense of humor.

Unfortunately, most of us confuse having a "good sense of humor" with being witty and sarcastic—at someone else's expense, as we see manifested by countless comedians and sit-coms. For instance, we see Groucho Marx, when introduced to a rather horse-faced woman, waggling his bushy eyebrows and saying:

> "I never forget a face, but in your case I'll make an exception."

The audience erupts with laughter—at the woman, who is the butt of the "clever" joke that makes fun of her physical appearance. This is an example of "laughing at" humor, which is not what happy couples mean by a sense of humor. They mean the capacity to "laugh with" one another. "Laughing at" humor usually hurts someone—although the expectation is that they will be a "good sport" and join in the laughter, concealing their pain. We are absolutely right to want to avoid this kind of hurtful humor.

That's hard to do at first, for most of what passes for "humor" in our culture is actually hostility—a "biting wit." Freud pointed out in an essay entitled "Wit and the Unconscious" that people who are afraid to express their anger directly will do so indirectly through jokes and witticisms. In this kind of "humor" there is always a butt to the joke whom the jokester is actually attacking.

Examples abound around us, so that we assume, quite incorrectly, that to be funny humor must be barbed. Think back to the cruel "humor" of childhood:

> "Hey, Four-Eyes! You wearin' Coke bottles on your nose?"

> "Fatty, Fatty, two-by-four, couldn't get through the bathroom door...."

It is not only the meanest children who will participate. Peer pressure is such that few will resist the group laugh and say, "That's not funny. It's cruel."

As we get a bit older, irony—the saying of the opposite of what we mean—becomes an effective weapon:

"Nice play, Shakespeare." (Said after someone is clumsy.)

These two traditions are supremely manifested in much British humor. In the famously acerbic *Black Adder* series, for example, the butler, the symbolically named Black Adder (played by Rowan Atkinson), who has a venomous tongue and is full of repressed rage at his lowly position in a hierarchical society, takes merciless shots at the Prince (Hugh Laurie) and the dogsbody Baldrick (Tony Robinson), both of whom are portrayed as morons. Black Adder calls them names, puts them down, outwits them, and is arrogantly superior. Yashi and I say, "He's so *mean!*" and order the next DVD. Freud would probably say we are gaining a vicarious revenge upon a society that makes us all feel like underlings. The revenge of the 99%.

Very popular in our culture are laughing-at jokes which demean an ethnic, sexual, or racial group:

Sven: How many Swedes does it take to change a light bulb?

Lars: Three. One to hold the light bulb and two to turn the ladder.

Notice that just about anyone could be substituted for "Swedes": Italians, blacks, blondes, women, etc. These putdowns are easily spotted, being politically incorrect at the current moment. Jokes that demean a single individual are still considered kosher.

Shakespeare has a character say that punning is the

lowest form of wit. I disagree with the Bard on that one—puns, as he himself knew well, often reveling in them, are often just fun. I would suggest that jokes that put down and laugh at another person are the lowest form of wit.

This form of "humor" can wound in many ways, directly with the naming or put-down, and then indirectly with the crazy-making aftermath if the "butt" challenges the joker by protesting that his or her feelings have been hurt. The almost invariable reply is:

> "Can't you take a joke?"

Or, more subtly:

> "I wasn't trying to hurt your feelings. That wasn't my intent at all."

In both instances the underlying message is that the butt is being an oversensitive butt-head for not seeing that the joker is absolutely innocent of any malicious intent. Since the intent is within the joker and since it is often disguised by layers of irony, the joker can semi-plausibly deny any culpability, which further wounds the butt for being "too sensitive."

Freud, however, busted the joker, pointing out that *all* such humor has a hostile intent at its core, even if the joker is unaware of that fact.

Many people delight in this "game" in which they can (a) put someone else down, (b) make them feel crazy and oversensitive by denying that that intended any hostility, and (c) appear to be all tender concern, the Nice Guy or Gal who would *never* do such a thing—and certainly won't cop to the hostility underneath the "joke." The butt soon starts wondering about his or her sanity.

So most "butts" just chuckle along and work up a real zinger to get the perpetrator back later. This breeds a spiral of vicious, cutting remarks which barely mask the hostility and can poison a relationship over time.

The same is true for relationships in which "practical jokes" are popular. He puts exploding devices in her cigarettes; she drops a worm into his spaghetti. The underlying anger may be more obvious in these jokes that involve physical acts.

Good Humor

So engulfed are we in hostile humor—verbal or practical—that you may be wondering what's left to joke about.

Compassionate humor never makes another person or group the butt of any joke. It doesn't name-call, put down, or demean in any way. If there is a butt, it is the joker, who tells the joke on himself, as did Mark Twain when he said:

> "Giving up smoking is quite easy. I've done it hundreds of times."

In this famous one-liner, Twain invites us to laugh at *his* foibles—and perhaps, through his, to reflect upon our own, as fallible humans who aspire to be better than we are. Such humor is *inclusive* rather than *exclusive*. Instead of an in-group laughing at an inferior out-group, we all laugh together at ourselves.

In my household, we have always had a similar orientation, as did my family of origin. We pun and joke a lot, but put-downs, sarcasm, and name-calling are off limits. If family members are carrying anger, I want them to express that directly rather than through a "joke." Then we can address the problem. Our "No put-downs" rule is as important to me as our "People are not for hitting" rule. In my life I have certainly been wounded at least as much by "humor" as by blows—and as a former boxer, football and lacrosse player I've taken a lot of blows. I am determined to have our home be safe from that kind of verbal abuse.

Instead, we look for ways to laugh *with* one another. When we find a good laugh, we record it in our Family Humor Book. It's a delight to go back and read this humorous history, as when my elder son made up the following riddle at age five:

Q: Why do rubber bands go boingey-boingey-boingey?
A: Because they have no ancestors.

At that point I figured he was the reincarnation of a Zen monk. But I couldn't imagine how he'd already learned the word "ancestors."

When every family member is on a daily hunt for something that is funny—a cartoon, a humorist's column, a joke—they tend to find more humor in life and laugh more. A simple psychological truth is that we will find what we are looking for. When we get together for the evening meal, we share the funny stories, cartoons, or jokes we're come across that day. It's great for the digestion. You might want to consider doing that in your own family or relationship. You can laugh a lot, and no one has hurt feelings. In fact, people need to feel safe in order to laugh fully, because laughing fully, like love, is an opening experience.

The Fear of Hurting People

From the prior section you can perhaps understand why many of us are cautious about risking hurting people with our sense of humor. Many of us have been hurt being the butt of someone's joke and we don't want to inflict that pain upon someone else. So what we can do is to make sure that we are using *inclusive* rather than *exclusive* humor. If you make a clear distinction between *laughing with* and *laughing at*, you won't need to be concerned.

Laughing With	Laughing At
1. Includes people	1. Excludes people
2. Puts others up	2. Puts others down
3. Goes for the jocular vein	3. Goes for the jugular vein
4. Caring	4. Contempt
5. Empathy	5. Lack of sensitivity
6. Brings people closer	6. Divides people
7. Choice to be the "butt"	7. No choice but to be "butt"
8. Builds confidence	8. Destroys self-esteem
9. Invites people	9. Excludes people
10. Leads to positive repartee	10. Leads to one-downsmanship
11. Can involve laughing at yourself	11. Laughs at others
12. Supportive	12. Sarcastic[30]

---

30 I wish to express my appreciation to Joel Goodman of The Humor Project for creating this list.

You might want to add to this list with your own ideas:
13,   13.

Exercise: How might you encourage a "laughing with" atmosphere in your relationship? How can you prevent hostile humor and sponsor more gentle humor?

Laughing with your Partner in Relationship

If you can laugh with your partner at your troubles, you'll always have something to laugh about together. Laughing will then shift your attitude toward your troubles and they won't seem so overwhelming. Anything that stresses us out in relationship—or in life—is an opportunity to laugh. Once we have that perspective, we can reframe the stress as an opportunity for humor.

A colleague tells the story of being in a serious argument with his partner in the kitchen. They were yelling at each other and getting red in the face. Frustrated past words, he grabbed an egg from the open carton on the counter, lifted it high in the air, and smashed it down on his forehead. As the goo ran down his face, they both collapsed in hysterics. The mood shifted from frustration to friendliness in an instant.

You don't have to look very hard to find humor around you, because nothing is funnier than reality. When the water main bursts, one tack you can take is to fret and get ulcers. Another is to laugh, take off your clothes, and play in the water.

Unintentional humor is everywhere, if you but keep your eyes open for it. Here's a message from a church bulletin. I find church bulletins a rich source of unintended humor:

> Here at St. Paul's we have a very active Young Mothers' Club. More experienced mothers meet with the new mothers to share expertise on diapering, breastfeeding, and tricks to put your baby to sleep, etc. If you wish to become a Young Mother, meet with Rev. Randy in his study after the sermon.

Laughter pops us out of our assumptions and our culturally-bound ways of seeing things.

While I was in Japan, I watched a Cary Grant movie in English with Japanese *katakana* subtitles. When Mr. Grant told his lovely leading lady that he loved her, the theater erupted in laughter. I was puzzled by this reaction.

"What's so funny?" I whispered to my Japanese companion.

"He told her he loved her!" Kazuko said, giggling uncontrollably behind one hand.

"What's so funny about that?" I asked.

"In Japan, we do not say it," she said. "If you love each other, you know it. If you don't, you also know it. It's silly to say something you both know."

My mouth dropped open. I thought of all the times I'd been badgered to say "it." I decided, with a sudden flash of insight, that the Japanese were right. (Though I still think it doesn't hurt to say it.)

Deep laughter is a *catharsis*, an emotional purging of the body and spirit. As such, it will clear out repressed feelings. It's healing to laugh—for the body, for the spirit, for your relationship. Let your laughter thrive.

Play

Once you've found ways to laugh together you're already playing. There's lots of confusion about play—clients often tell me that they don't know how to play, then go on to speak with obvious animation about their work or their garden. I think advertising promotes the idea that play must include doing something mindless and frivolous, parachuting into Puerto Vallarta in bikinis and leaping around like hopheads in the surf. Many of us think of "play" as what the ads tell us to do while asking, "Are we having fun yet?" If you ain't havin' fun, you ain't playin'.

Play is what you enjoy.

Whereas laughter, which can be playful, is the opposite of serious, much play is very serious. Watch children at play. They go about "playing house" with straight faces. Heaven help the "baby" who disobeys "Mommy." Their level of focus is very high. In fact, they display many of the characteristics of adults engaged in meaningful work. Someone has said that play is children's work.

For adults just the opposite can be true: Meaningful work can be play. Some adults enjoy their work vastly. Joseph Campbell did what he loved and managed to make a good living from it. His advice to people is to "Follow your bliss." Fortunate is the man or woman who gets paid for doing what he or she loves to do. Malik and LaVonne really loved their work. They felt fulfilled knowing they were making America more democratic and just.

"What we can do," LaVonne suggested, "is to conceptualize

what we do as play. We are, after all, playing the game of politics. That would help us not be so damn grim about it."

Malik thought that was a great idea.

"It's like playing 'Warcraft,'" he said, referring to a popular on-line game that he also enjoyed. "You have to figure out the tricks and work-arounds."

Make a List of What You Enjoy

When you are listing what sources of play you have in your life, don't forget work, if you indeed love it, if you leap out of bed eager to get to the job.

What else do you really enjoy doing? Take a sheet of paper and jot down as many activities that you can think of in the next few minutes. Here's the beginning of my list, to give you some ideas:

Sleeping	Dreaming
Making love	Eating
Showering, bathing	Writing
Reading	Seeing my clients
Teaching	Doing research
Gardening	Playing softball, basketball
Backpacking	Fishing
Splitting wood	Building things
Aerobics, dancing	Swimming in a mountain lake
Body surfing at the ocean	Skiing
Watching movies & plays	Listening to music, singing
Being with my children	Getting together with friends

Sipping cocoa beside the fire on a cold night…

When I'm playing, I find that I'm very focused while experiencing a sense of effortlessness. If I have to "work" at fun, I'm not really having fun. Here I am, skiing down Mt. Disney at Sugarbowl. All my attention is in the immediate present. I am not wondering whether the economy will recover or whether a new war has begun somewhere. I'm aware only of the brilliant white of the snow, the dark greens of the evergreens, the feel of the sun and wind on my face, the swish of my skis cutting into the powder, the way the terrain changes beneath my boots. At the same time I feel like a big bird, a raptor effortlessly gilding down the mountain. My body swings back and forth across the fall line in curving turns, and everything—the day, the snow, my body, my mind, my spirit—seems to be in perfect harmony. I experience a sense of inner peace.[31]

The same thing happens when I'm making love or reading a good book. Effortlessness, oneness, inner tranquility. Therefore, I don't think it's so much *what* we are doing that is or is not playful so much as *how* we are doing it. I could be working at skiing. I can be playing while writing this book. As a matter of fact, I am having a lot of fun writing today.

Play is what brings a bodily feeling of pleasure. You might enjoy doing a crossword puzzle, racking your brain, but the feeling of pleasure is in your body.

Try this fun **exercise:** Take some crayons and a big piece of drawing paper. With your *non-dominant* hand, draw a picture of yourself as a child. On the back side of the same paper, using the same hand, make a list of what you loved to do as a child.

---

31   See "Slomo" at http://nyti.ms/1gIRvD7

Now, compare this list to the one you just did as an adult. What do you notice? Is there anything on the child's list you'd like to bring back?

A Tale of Two Couples

Scott is looking forward to sailing on Sunday. He's loaded the catamaran onto the carrier, he's gassed the truck; he even remembered to purchase a lake usage permit ahead of time to make sure he'd get on the water. Jackie has packed a lunch and iced a nice bottle of Zin. They set the alarm for 4 a.m. even though they aren't in bed till almost midnight.

When the alarm explodes they aren't feeling much like getting up, but they drag themselves out of bed and groggily drive out to the lake slurping coffee from stainless steel mugs. Of course they spill hot coffee on their legs—and their Gucci shorts—and are screaming at each other long before the boat's even in the water.

They've bought into all of the Mad Ave accouterments of "fun" but aren't having any. The "correct" image was in mind but the body is tired, irritable, and is getting sunburned. When they discovered neither of them had brought the sunscreen, each of them blamed the other.

On the same Sunday morning, Zack and Molly slept in, awoke making love, and slept some more. Around eleven Zack squeezed some oranges and they sipped o.j. in bed while discussing what to do with their day. They began with a shower together, scrubbing each other's backs, and then went out for brunch with some friends. The friends invited them to play some volleyball on the beach court down at the lake and then take a swim. They threw some towels and sunscreen in the car and drove to the lake, singing along with the 60s station on the way.

They didn't keep score in their volleyball game but had fun anyway—or maybe because nobody had to lose. As they swam about near the beach, they noticed a beautiful couple in Gucci shorts sailing a cat up the lake. They envied them just a little, thinking they must be having a really great time in their sailboat and expensive clothes, but then, somehow, playing underwater tag with their friends, they forgot all about them.

A Few Ideas for Cultivating Play and Laughter

1. Support each other in laughing with rather than laughing at.
2. Observe daily reality to find what's humorous. Share funny events of the day in the evening.
3. Keep a record of funny events and stories in a family humor book.
4. Laugh together. Begin each day with five minutes of laughing. Use a laugh tape to get you started, if necessary.
5. Hunt for funny films, tapes, books, comedians, cartoons, etc., and share them with each other. Support comedians of the "laugh with" school.
6. Compare your "Play" lists and circle the activities that you both enjoy. Do at least one of these activities together each week.
7. Take turn structuring fun dates. Partner A makes the

plans and tells you what to wear (if anything). You then enter the experience step by step. Next week Partner B makes the plans.

An example: Sam told Sally to dress casually and drove her out to the ball park for a game. He explained the game, told her anecdotes about the players and their love lives, and bought her hot dogs and lemonade. Afterwards, he took her to the batting cage and they tried to hit slow-pitched softballs.

The next week, Sally had him rent a tux and showed up in a slinky black dress. She took him to Chez Panisse for an exquisite dinner and then to the opera. Sam had always said he hated opera, but the way Sally extemporized in their private box gave him new insights into the musical world.

8. Role play. Act out who you always wanted to be but were afraid to risk. At home, Sally had Sam rent the same tux (he's thinking of buying one) and he let the James Bond in him emerge. Sally dolled herself up as a Russian spy on the make. Her attempt at a Russian accent was hilarious. You can imagine the rest.

9. Find your own ways to play and laugh together.

Afterword

As you focus more on safe play and laughter in your relationship, you'll find more spontaneity and unpredictability permeating your time together. Play and laughter jar us out of our human tendency to fall into predictable routines. When we're mired in ruts, we grow bored. When we're bored, a new relationship or a solo trip to Nepal has a strong allure. When we're having fun, we want to come back for more.

Use your little gray cells to create more fun in your relationship. You'll start looking forward to your time together in the evening, even if only to share the joke you heard that day. Your relationship will be less serious—and a lot more fun. When you're having so much fun at home, playing and laughing together, you won't need to be hunting for fun in all the wrong places.

CHAPTER 6:
EXPLORE INNER SPACE TOGETHER

There are more things in heaven and earth
than are dreamt of in our philosophy.
—William Shakespeare's Hamlet

Most of us confine our lives to the glittering surface of things: What's on TV tonight, those damn taxes, and how it's even possible that our best friends are getting a divorce. And why not stay with what we know? It's what we grew up with. Few of us were taught how to explore Inner Space—or even that it exists.

We tend to believe that what we can see or touch or perceive consciously is what is "real"—and that what we can't isn't. The result is that the maps we carry in our heads about what constitutes "reality" have a few markings in one corner and vast blank spaces stamped with the words "Unknown" or "Here there be dragons."

I remember a lovely Finnish movie, whose title I've forgotten, in which a boy insists to a shaman that what is invisible doesn't exist. In a flash, the shaman claps one hand over the boy's mouth and with the other pinches his nostrils closed. The boy can't breathe. In a panic, he struggles wildly. After a few more seconds the shaman releases him.

"The air is invisible," the shaman says, "yet without it you will die."

The boy gets the point.

In the same way, we live our lives surrounded by and

infused with myriad invisible forces that are as real for us as air. If we ignore them, a part of us will suffocate. If we explore them together as a couple, we will discover deep connections that most other relationships lack. We will also come back into touch with the magic of this Universe.

Inner Space has many pseudonyms. Freud called it the unconscious. Emerson called it the Oversoul. A Christian, God or the Holy Spirit. A Hindu the *atman*. What signpost we attach to it is of little importance. In this chapter I will point you toward some paths into Inner Space that are more psychological: Mindfulness, deep feelings, dreams, the drum journey, and past life regression. In the next we will explore some spiritual paths, although this division between spirit and psyche, as you will see, starts to become arbitrary along the way.

How do you feel right now, hearing that we might be beginning such an exploration together? Excited? Frightened? A bit of both?

I suggest that you take a few minutes to set this book aside and ask a friend to read the following exercise to you. If you don't have a friend handy, you can read it into a recording device to play for yourself.

Semi-darken the room, lie down on a comfortable surface, close your eyes and breathe deeply.

Exercise: Imagine that you and your partner (if you don't have one yet, imagine one) are heading downriver in an inflated yellow rubber raft steered by a competent guide. What does your guide look like? Gender, hair color, eyes, body type, clothing. Your guide assures you that this river is readily navigable. Right here, the river is broad and you glide along in a smooth current. Take a few moments to see the details of your guide and the flora and fauna of the riverbank.

Up ahead you hear rapids. Your guide tells you to pick up broad-bladed paddles and to back water to hold yourself in the middle of the river, which is narrowing into a small canyon. Now you see the whitewater churning around underwater boulders. Your raft begins picking up speed. How do you feel?

As you enter the rapids, your raft lurches left, then right, then spins completely around. How is that for you? Exciting? Scary? Both? Your guide is yelling above the din for you to paddle forward hard. As you do so your raft comes head up and plunges through the center of the rapids— and then into smooth and calmer waters. You slow, and your guide tells you to take a breather. Are you relieved at having a break? Or disappointed that it's over so soon?

What do you imagine awaits you downriver?

You might wish to take a few minutes to write down some notes on what you saw and how you felt during this imagery.

How is this imaginative experience of whitewater rafting like exploring Inner Space? The feelings that come up for you are probably similar. What about the specifics? Take your guide, for instance. Did you feel a bit more secure, knowing you have with you a guide who's traveled this river before? In fact, one part of your personal Inner Space contains a Guide who is always with you and who can help you face the excitements of exploration. By all means, take him or her along with you on future adventures. You might want to confer with your Guide on other occasions, including assisting you in making decisions in external reality, such as which car to buy or whether this person is good mate potential. As you do so, you will become more mindful of how to make better decisions for yourself. But what do I mean by being "mindful"?

Mindfulness

We can be mindful of what is within as well as what's outside us. Most of us are more familiar with what's outside. Right now I'm looking at my monitor screen and then the snow on the gentle hillside out my window; I can hear the fire crackling in the woodstove and smell the bacon frying. You will notice that we become outwardly mindful mainly through our senses. That's easy for me. Harder is to become mindful of what I'm feeling inside. For other people it's just the opposite.

Whenever we engage an inner Observer to notice what we are aware of in the present moment, we are being mindful.

You might remember the "Now I am aware…." exercise from *Real Relationship*. Take a minute to set this book down and to become aware of what grabs your attention, both within and without.

On which arena, inside or outside, do you tend to focus more?

As you paused in your reading in the last two exercises to check in on what you were feeling, you became more mindful of those feelings. That is the essence of inner *mindfulness*—becoming more and more aware of what is happening within you. Because most of us didn't get much practice in becoming mindful growing up, we will tend to feel awkward at it at first. As with anything, it takes focused practice. One of my clients, who works at a computer, programmed that computer to chime at him every hour and to flash onto his screen the question

WHAT AM I FEELING INSIDE RIGHT NOW?

If you simply keep asking yourself that question several times a day, you will become more mindful of your rich inner life.

You need not strain yourself at this task. Check in, first, to how you are feeling *physically*. Scan yourself from head to toes, as if you are getting an MRI. Do you have a headache or not? How do your eyes feel? Is your neck stiff or relaxed? Throat? How does your breathing feel to you? Your heartbeat? Continue down your entire body.

Then ask yourself: Do I feel basically good in my physical body or bad? If good, take a deep breath and enjoy the good feeling. Breathe into it.

If bad, locate precisely where in your body you feel a pain or tension or dis-ease. Breathe more deeply into that part of your body. Get a deeper sense of what might be going on.

For instance, right now I can feel a slightly painful stiffness in the back of my head and upper neck. That area seems to want to stretch. As I breathe into it and stretch it the area begins to loosen and not hurt so much. I'm guessing I might have tensed up trying to figure out how to make that text box I just made.

What feeling label might I apply, as a guesstimate, for the emotion contained in my neck? Remember (from Chapter 7 in *Real Relationship*) that it's probably *sad mad glad or afraid*.

Well, it hurts, so I can rule out *glad*.

I don't feel afraid. So it's either sad or mad. Which?

Hmm. Probably some of each. I'm sad that I'm not more computer literate, and I'm frustrated that placing the text box took me so long. Grr.

While the next step is what I'm going to do about it, I'm going to stop the investigation here because I want to focus here on being mindful rather than doing anything about it. (Too many of us cut off our mindfulness by immediately moving into Fix-It mode.)

I now know that I have a painful neck and that I'm equal parts sad and mad.

If I wish, or if she asks, I can tell my partner, "I have a stiff neck from the frustration of trying to build a text box. I'm sad I'm not more computer literate."

Now she has a deeper and more accurate understanding of me than if I'd said "Fine." It's not that "Fine" is a lie; I can have a stiff neck and also be fine.

Most of the women I see in couples' counseling tell me that if they ask their men how they feel they always get the same answer: "Fine."

This reply frustrates these women because they can guess from the nonverbal signals they're seeing that the guy is far from fine.

What's going on in the guys? When they hear this (for most of us) dreaded question, it provokes a constellation of responses that tends to overwhelm us and strike most of us dumb.

First, after years of schooling in which we were put on the spot by a variety of questions, we tend to get stage fright and become embarrassed about what the "right" answer is, especially when "Fine" doesn't cut it.

In fact, "Fine" is a fine answer for most guys most of the time. We've been acculturated to be fine. Unless we're hungry or horny or have just smashed a thumb with the hammer, we're fine. But for most women, that's an inadequate response, especially when there's a mismatch between what he's saying and how he looks.

Some men freeze up at this question and its siblings and can't even speak. Other men offer glib distractions, such as, "I'm just happy to be around you, baby."

Second, when a man really cares about you, the last thing in the world he wants to do is to upset you. He sees his main job as keeping you happy. He'll slay a dragon for you, or fix your leaky faucet. So when he gets this question he's never learned how to answer—and then sees your frustration—he panics.

Of course he can't admit, even to himself, that he's panicking. Since we were very little boys we have been told "Big boys aren't scaredy-cats." So he says "Fine" or nothing, hoping to avoid the inquisition. When that doesn't fly, his panic magnifies and he starts looking for a way out. What he literally cannot do is answer the question honestly. He has no idea how to.

Most women, in contrast, can tell me how they feel moment by moment. Or at least they think they can. They often mix up how they feel (inside) and what they perceive (outside). So when the guy says, "Fine," he often gets hit with, "Bullshit. I feel you're angry."

Now he's really confused and terrified. There is no happy outcome ahead that he can see.

What women (and men) can do is to get clear about the difference between a feeling and a perception. What men (and some women) can do is to become more mindful of how they feel.

We become more mindful through practice. Set the timer on your watch and, once every hour ask yourself "Am I sad mad glad or afraid right now?"

If you find you are honestly glad ("Fine") most of the time, enjoy your bliss. But also push yourself to look a little below the surface to investigate such feelings as:

1. Was I a tiny bit irritated by how I can seldom meet her standards of tidiness?
2. Was I a tiny bit irritated that he left the toilet seat up, again?
3. When I saw that attractive woman/man at the next table, did I get a tiny bit nervous that my partner would notice and be annoyed with me?
4. When she/he left me alone for the weekend, did I feel a little twinge of sadness?
5. Do I feel my heart swell with love when I first see her/him gussied up for a date?

By simply paying more attention to these blips on your radar screen you will become more mindful of what it is you are feeling. Then you will have an answer to the dreaded question that your partner will recognize as authentic. However, don't be surprised if it's still difficult for you to make your speaking apparatus form the words and articulate them. It will take practice to overcome this block as well.

As you learn to recognize what you are feeling and to share that with your partner, you build a bridge between you that grows stronger with every journey across it. You are presenting more of yourself to your partner and thereby offering more for him or her to connect to. As you do so, you will gradually get past your belief that some feelings are "negative" and be able to acknowledge them honestly as facts of life rather than fearing them as grounds for divorce or proof that you are a defective human being.

Exploring Feelings Together

Once you begin to have some sense of what it is you are feeling moment to moment, you have the opportunity to explore deeper feelings together with your partner. Since I have covered this process in some detail in Chapter 9 of *Real Relationship*, I'm going to simply refer you to that source rather than repeating myself.

Please don't overlook this powerful means of cementing a deeper and stronger relationship: It is *the* most potent means for doing so.

Sharing the Dreamtime Together

I find it fascinating that as a culture we dismiss our dreams as irrelevant, as in "It's only a dream" or "He's such a dreamer." Many people don't even remember their dreams, much less honor them as very important.

Cultures that honor their dreams, such as the Senoi, have almost no incidents of murder, theft, rape, or assault.[32] Is it possible that when we honor the unconscious we need not act it out?

Historically we have a long tradition of honoring the Dreamtime. The Bible has several stories illustrating the importance of dreams, including the famous one of how Joseph saved Egypt from famine. Freud maintained dreams were the royal road to healing the psyche. Jung constructed his theory of archetypes around them. Kerkule was given the chemical structure of the benzene ring in a daydream. And many of us first met our loved one in a dream.

I suggest that you and your partner begin exploring and sharing the Dreamtime together. Doing so will connect you in the richness of the unconscious.

Some people tell me they don't dream. That is a wonderful example of a shocking if widespread lack of mindfulness. Just because you don't remember something doesn't mean it didn't happen. We all dream. Sleep lab studies have proven this over and again. If you are a doubter, spend a night in a sleep lab. Or ask your partner to watch you while you sleep and wake you when your eyelids begin to flutter.

You say you seldom remember your dreams? That's "normal." But once we begin paying attention to our dreams, it will become normal to remember more of them.

If you want to catch your dreams, set your intention to do so by placing a pen and paper on your bedside table. When you first wake up, don't even sit up. Roll over and

---

32   See S. Kaplan-Williams, *The Jungian Senoi Dreamwork Manual* (1988).

make some notes on your dream or draw a picture of it.

My dreams are elusive. If I tell myself "This dream I'm having is so clear—of course I'll remember it!" and then do anything else but write it down, I'll lose it, 99 times out of 100.

Once you begin catching your dreams, have a Dream Circle each morning. Each person in your household or in your backpacking group takes a minute or two to recount his or her dream. Don't *analyze* or *interpret* anyone's dreams, your own included. Focus instead on how you *feel* in the dream, your own or someone else's. Dreams are usually pictures of feelings. Simply open yourself to the power of them.

Notice patterns that develop over time. Yashi and I delight in how often our separate dreams will contain a common theme—last night we were both on the Rive Gauche in Paris, for instance. Over the course of the day, be open to having a dream image or feeling pop back up into your consciousness.

Many dreams will be reorganizations of something that happened the day before. (The evening before we dreamed of Paris, we had watched the movie *Midnight in Paris*.) At other times a dream will reach out and grab you with a power that is almost frightening. For example, Yashi had a dream about two mountain lions trying to get into our house. She was terrified that they meant to eat her. Jung called such dreams, which are both scary and seem to possess a spiritual nature, *numinous*. While you might want to work with any dream, a numinous dream usually holds vast riches. What follows is the most effective way you can mine the riches in a dream. It was developed by the great Gestalt therapist, Fritz Perls:

Exercise in Dreamwork: You can do this alone or with a partner. If the latter, the partner just listens and provides a safe container for you. All you need is two chairs or other sitting places, such as pillows or rocks. Sit down in one place, close your eyes, and breathe deeply (I hope you're beginning to notice how important it is that we pay attention to our breath and enlarge it). Bring the dream up into consciousness. Begin at the beginning and speak the dream *aloud*, even if you're alone, retelling it *in the present tense* as you see it unfolding. Doing so will help you put yourself more vividly into the dream. Speak slowly. Recount details. Allow yourself to feel deeply— slow down even more when you encounter a feeling. Breathe. Express the feeling: Say, "I'm scared!" when you see the zombie reaching for your neck. Follow each feeling as far as it will go.

Now choose one person, place, or thing from your dream to *dialog* with. Pick whatever flirts with you first, but there's really no right or wrong choice—any feature will do. Yashi might pick one of the mountain lions. Still with closed eyes, she visualizes the lion, as best she can, lounging in the chair across from her, describing it, out loud, as thoroughly as she can. Then she addresses the lion directly, saying how she feels about it and what she's curious about.

Now, keeping her eyes closed, she moves from the first chair to the second and sits down in the mountain lion's spot. She takes a few moments to imagine herself inside the lion. How does she breathe as a lion? How does it feel to have big sharp teeth and long sharp claws? To have such powerful muscles?

Next, she gives the mountain lion (or the zombie, or the Eiffel Tower, or whatever she has picked to dialog with) voice and speaks through that dream image, across to her "self." (I'll tell you why I put that in quotes later.) She *becomes* lion as fully as she can and speaks from that point of view, until she feels finished.

Then she switches back to the first chair, takes a moment to re-enter the Yashi of the dream, and, if she wishes, responds back to the lion. She continues switching chairs and the voice dialog for as long as she wishes, noticing what happens to the relationship between Yashi and lion as she does so.

When she thinks she's finished, she asks herself this important question: *What part of me might the mountain lion represent?*

I want to pause the exercise for a few minutes to discuss it a bit. As Perls pointed out, and as Freud postulated prior to Perls, all parts of our dreams are parts of the dreamer. (While I don't agree that this is *always* the case, it is a fruitful assumption to begin with.) Therefore, the mountain lion is a part of Yashi's psyche. So is the "self" in the dream—a *part* of Yashi, not the whole Yashi.

*In fact, and in a parallel manner, the conscious "self" that we construct and **believe** to be who we are is but a small part of who we **actually** are.*

Some readers will be shocked by this statement and want to argue with me. Others will yawn and think, "Does he really imagine we don't all know that already?"

If you are in the latter group, please tolerate me for a bit. If in the former, please tolerate me for a bit.

I don't have the space here to "prove" this fact to you. I will, however, tell you the lovely Zen Buddhist story of the monk who dreamed he was a butterfly. He had beautiful wings and soared effortlessly through the air. When he awakened he was unsure: "Am I a man who dreamed he was a butterfly? Or a butterfly who is now dreaming he is a man?"

If we accept the premise that both states—waking and dreaming—are "real" for just a moment, what are the consequences of such acceptance? One is that I now see myself as much vaster than I did before. A second is that I now have a much larger Self from which to connect to a loved one. If she also has such a larger Self, we multiply the possibilities of our interaction and connection.

Can you see the advantages for the purpose of co-creating deeper bonds?

As Yashi dialogs with the mountain lion of her dream and then asks, "What part of me is a mountain lion?" and answers "Wow, that's a pretty powerful part! Grrr!" she stretches her sense of who she is. She might want to get up from her chair and move like a lion around the room, unsheathing her claws and roaring. As she feels the lioness part of herself, she gets to experience this powerful part that she had to distance her conscious self from early in life when her parents made it unwelcome. Over time, she denied that she had such power and *shrank her sense of self down to what was societally acceptable.* As she begins to accept that she is part lion, she finds that she is better able to stand her ground and to ask for what she wants. She finds herself less fearful of bullies. Through the dream and the dreamwork she is regaining a lost part of herself.

As her partner, I am delighted to have her asking directly for what she wants and being able to stand toe-to-toe with me in a dispute. I don't want to spend a lifetime with someone who can't be my equal in that way. On her side, Yashi acknowledges that not being able to stand up for herself led her to grow suffocated in former relationships, which she then had to leave.

"It's scary for me to confront you," she says, "but I know I have to do it if I want to avoid holding resentments. When I stockpile a stack of resentments, I want to get out of Dodge."

I thank her for her bravery. When I tell her it's also scary for me to confront her, at first she doesn't believe me.

"You stand up for yourself and ask for what you want better than anyone I know," she says. "It seems easy for you."

It isn't easy for me. It's often downright terrifying. But I likewise know that if I "go along to get along" I will soon resent the relationship.

As we both support each other to re-own split off parts of ourselves and to be real in our relationship, we build deep, strong bonds that would not be easy to rebuild with someone else.

Are you beginning to see why this work is important to your relationship?

Though we come into this life as golden balls of light, we are soon reshaped into square adobe bricks that fit into the house our caretakers want to build. We become mere shards of our former whole Selves. We now have the opportunity to re-own our purloined parts and to work toward reconstructing ourselves as our true Selves. Our relationships are freeways to doing so, if we are willing to re-form them as such.

Back to the dreamwork:

Exercise (continued): Whatever you chose to work with first, as Yashi did the mountain lion, is just one part of the dream. You can take any portion of it to dialog with. You can dialog with a house, a lake, a car. Animate or inanimate makes no difference for the dreamwork. In any one dream, or even dream fragment, you will find treasures. Then, if you wish, you can work from the dream outward. If this dream were to continue, what would happen next? What would I want to happen next? What would I most fear happening next? Your possibilities are infinite.

By sharing your dreams with mutual respect, you will discover an entire new archipelago where you will get to know yourselves and each other and to connect in ways you never dreamed of in waking life.

The Drum Journey

Another potent means of accessing Inner Space is the drum journey. Along with hallucinogenic plants, the drum was one of humankind's first means of accessing the psycho-spiritual world. It was the primary tool in what many anthropologists call the world's earliest religion: shamanism. Shamanism sprang up all over in the globe, in all cultures that we know of, as a means of connecting directly to spirit. However, it is not really a religion in the modern sense of that word, for it has no dogma, no hierarchical structures with a single pope or guru or ayatollah at the top, and no inquisitions to ensure conformity of belief. Of course any spiritual practice will have its power-hungry abusers who will try to corral others. I suggest you shun anyone who is certain of the way psycho-spiritual reality should be for you.

I find it interesting that identical or very similar spiritual practices and discoveries came into being separately in many different cultures and at about the same time. This fact would seem to support Carl Jung's belief that human beings everywhere are endowed with a "collective unconscious," which also accounts for the parallels between the mythic stories that our ancestors created. If all humans share the same unconscious material, the exploration of it will help us understand how alike we are.

The use of the drum in that exploration is almost universal. While there are some variations—such as the use of click sticks among the aborigines of Australia—the early discovery was that a rhythmic beat at a certain rate (around 120-140 beats per minute) opened the doors of perception to unconscious/spiritual material. Modern neuroscience has shown that what then occurs is the lifting of the gating mechanism in the hippocampus that usually screens out such material. In our daily lives, when we need our brain for less esoteric matters, such as figuring out how to use the toaster or how much we owe the IRS, interference by such material can be distracting. In fact, if it happens frequently, a modern psychiatrist might assign a label of schizophrenia. Many shamans, who are revered in their own cultures as beings of great spiritual insight, would receive such a label from a conventional shrink.

If you are someone who enjoys rock music, you may have already experienced the non-drug "high" that can come from the steady beat of the drum at about this rate. If you are simultaneously dancing to the beat, you might have entered a kind of altered state, which is commonly sought among many peoples who practice what anthropologists call the "trance dance." The purpose of the trance dance, like the drum journey, is to open the doors of perception to the spirit world—and to feel pretty good while doing so.

If you want to do a drum journey together, there are a couple ways you might experiment with. There are tapes and discs made precisely for that purpose. You can purchase one of these, load it into a suitable playing device, lie flat on your back on something comfortable, shut your eyes, and go with the beat. The advantage of this method is that you can both journey together.

I like the second method, which requires a drum and someone to beat it. Yashi and I take turns being the drummer and the Explorer. The Explorer lies down in a semi-darkened room (or on her sleeping bag out in the nighttime forest), closes her eyes, and rides the drumbeat. Shamanic peoples believe that the skin of the animal used to make the drum enables the hearer to ride that particular animal into the spirit world. Here's a fun beginning drum journey that can help you initiate a connection with an animal ally:

Before you start the drumbeat, lie down flat on your back on some relatively comfortable surface and let yourself see a forest scene in detail: See and smell the trees, the flowers, the grasses, and any water that might be there. The Drummer strikes the drum four times, to honor the

Four Directions, and then begins the steady drumming of about two beats per second. Settle into the beat and let yourself be open to whatever animal comes to you. Unless it is an insect, don't shop for an animal—take the first one who comes. (If it's an insect, respectfully decline and send it on its way.)

Look carefully at your animal helper to notice his or her qualities. Look into their eyes. How do you feel about having this particular helper come to you? Greet them respectfully.

Your animal helper wants to help you. He or she may say something to you, perhaps telepathically, or present you with a gift, or take you on an adventure to show you something. Accept this aid gratefully.

When the Drummer wishes to stop, he or she will stop the steady beat and strike the drum four times, then beat it very rapidly for about a minute. This is the signal for you to return to commonplace reality. Thank your animal ally for coming to you and giving you this experience. Come back through the forest that you saw in the beginning and return to your bodily awareness, the quick drumbeat, and the feel of your back contacting the surface you're lying on.

The Drummer will conclude with four more final, slow beats. You are now fully awake, refreshed, and invigorated. When you feel ready, open your eyes, sit up, take pencil and paper and jot down a few notes about your experience. If you wish, tell your partner some of the highlights.

I love many of the elements of the shamanic worldview, as I have learned them from my mentor, Don Tomas, who himself studied in both the Lakota and Huichol traditions. The first is that the Universe is out to do us good. Your animal allies, who come to you from the Spirit World, truly wish to assist you. In return, they ask two things: That you treat them with respect, showing gratitude for their help, and that you will, from time to time, lend them your body so they can remember what if feels like to be embodied. You do so by allowing them to dance you.

An enjoyable way of doing so is to put on a drumbeat or some music you love to dance to, then imagine (if that is the right word) that your animal ally is inhabiting your body as you let him or her move to the beat through your body. You can do this by yourself or with your partner. When you dance in this way in the same space as your partner it is very different from dancing *with* your partner, but it is meaningful and bonding nonetheless. Try it to see how you like it.

The more frequently you dance your animal, the closer the relationship will become. The more frequently you go on drum journeys, the deeper your connection to the Spirit World will become. Each time, your animal ally will show you more of that world.

From a psychological perspective, what you are doing is exploring your unconscious and connecting to archetypal figures in it.

From a shamanic perspective, you are journeying into the Spirit World and gaining knowledge that will help you to be more successful on your Earthwalk. From this perspective, we are spiritual beings who are presently walking the Earth in bodily form. As we make this Earthwalk we can benefit immensely from allies in the Spirit World.

Notice that these are simply parallel ways of describing

the same experience. Which view sounds like more fun to you? Is your animal helper an archetype from the collective unconscious? Or is it an actual being from the Spirit World?

How a Drum Journey Can Yield Information

After Yashi and I had been dating for a little over half a year, we felt that we'd like to live together. However, we also had our own children to consider, and the move Yashi and her daughter would need to make from their home (and school) in Fresno. We spoke to our children about the idea, and they gave us favorable feedback. We then brainstormed on a wide variety of possibilities, but nothing felt quite right to us.

Finally Yashi suggested that we do a drum journey to gain information from the Spirit World. I drummed and she journeyed. When she sat up she seemed discontent. I should tell you that this happened prior to her mountain lion dream of the previous section.

"All I got," she sighed, "was a new animal. A tawny mountain lion came to me and took me for a ride out across some gently rolling hills covered with oaks. I've never had a mountain lion come to me before. I don't see that that has any connection to our question."

Although I didn't either, I thought we could see what, if anything, was available that might suit our rather complex needs for four bedrooms and an office. While Yashi went off to a rental agency to see what they might have, I went through the local papers with a marking pen. There was nothing suitable in the papers at all.

Yashi came back similarly discouraged.

"The agency had almost nothing," she said. "The only possibility—and it seems like a long shot—is way out in Chicago Park. It's got four bedrooms and a separate office over the garage, but it's way too expensive for us."

I asked to see the description. It read something like this:

FOR RENT: Hand-crafted solar home (4 BRS, 3 BA, hot tub) on twenty wooded acres with a large pond. Separate apartment over three-car garage. Large front deck with 270-degree view. 15465 Mt. Lion Road, Chicago Park.

When I read the address the hairs on the back of my neck stood up. Yashi had somehow missed it. When I pointed it out she said, "Ohmygod!" and we both raced for the car.

We loved the property at first sight. It was on an oak-covered hilltop with an exhilarating wide-angle view; we could witness both sunrises and sunsets all year round and we knew we'd love sleeping out on the deck under the stars. The pond was clean and swimmable. The apartment over the separate garage made a good office space for us to work in, though it lacked handicapped access. And while the architecture of the house was a bit of a jumble, each of the kids had a bedroom downstairs and we had the upstairs master bedroom and there was a lovely glass hothouse across the front of the building where plants would grow year round.

The only drawback was that the rent the owner was asking was much higher than we could afford. We told him frankly that we loved the property but could only pay two-thirds of what he wanted.

"Golly," he said, scratching his head, "I was gonna hold

out for my price, but there's something about you guys that makes me want to have you live here...."

And that's how we got our house on Mountain Lion Road at the price we could afford.

You can, of course, point out that the mountain lion who came to Yashi in the drum journey and the address on that property we found that day could have been a bizarre coincidence. I'd encourage you to compute the probability. And if that were the only such "coincidence" that I'd ever experienced through a drum journey or a feeling session, I might even agree with you. However, once you have witnessed many such "coincidences," you lose your skepticism—and even your belief in coincidence.

Many Native American languages lack any word for "coincidence." Shamanic peoples tend to accept such felicitous occurrences as the workings of the Great Mystery. The Universe, you see, is out to do us good. Carl Jung called it *synchronicity*. Among the participants in AA, the phrase is: "Let go and let God." We need only open ourselves to that possibility.

Exploring Inner Space tends to stretch our understanding of what is possible. We'll investigate an even more mind-boggling possibility next.

Can We Explore Past Lives Together?

You say you don't believe in the possibility that you lived before this lifetime? I didn't either. I'd been raised in the Christian belief that we live once, then go to heaven or hell. I'm embarrassed to admit that, in a quite unscientific manner, I dismissed the possibility of past lives because many established thinkers pooh-poohed that possibility. If I had been truly scientific, I would have thought, "Well, let me explore this concept and see what the proof is, one way or the other."

As often happens for me, the initial shaking of the smug edifice of my philosophy came not from research but from experience. Once I'd had the eye-opening experience, I was motivated to pursue the research.

It was actually a two part experience. The first occurred in 1973 while I was in primal therapy. Through that exploration of my deepest feelings, I had already had my formerly narrow concept of Reality stretched and deepened. More on that later. One day I was in deep feelings around my belief that I should be responsible for other people's lives. I remembered being the commanding officer of Harvard Army ROTC, a proctor in prep school, and the eldest of four children, often left in charge of my siblings. Seemingly out of nowhere a rather surprising "movie" began to play before my closed eyes: I was on the pitching deck of a horse-headed Viking ship sailing through gray, stormy seas under a dark gray sky. Ice was forming on the ropes and spars. Some of the hawsers had torn loose and were flapping violently. The sail was furled and the bare mast looked naked. I was standing on the quarterdeck beside the helmsman, who struggled to hold the tiller true. My crew, bundled in furs against the icy cold, was trying to batten down the loose rigging and to bail out the hold. Every detail was as vivid as if it were an actual movie.

I somehow knew that I was the captain of the vessel and that the fate of my entire crew was in my hands. I was afraid that, as we were being driven northward by winds and currents, we were about to become locked in ice.

The next scene of the "movie" was terrible: We were icebound and I was so cold that my shivering—in the warm room at the Berkeley Center—was so violent that it jerked me out of the experience.

As I lay on the mat, shivering uncontrollably and gasping for breath, I wondered: Had I just experienced a piece of a past life? Or had my mind created a symbolic representation of my deep sense of responsibility and where it could lead me? I couldn't be sure. What I did know was that I had always taken what I saw as my responsibilities to my fellow human beings very seriously, often to a fault, and I resolved to examine that tendency more carefully in the future. In fact, simply having had that experience freed me tremendously from being overly responsible. I resolved to let go of being the big brother or the commanding officer henceforth.

I Move On to Research

That seemed benefit enough from the startling "movie" I had witnessed. I went on with my life, a bit lighter in spirit and action, and less sure that I'd never lived before.

I did some research into past lives and was intrigued by what I discovered. Dr. Ian Stephenson at the University of Virginia decided to collect the evidence to see where it pointed. He studied thousands of people in several countries who believed they could remember a prior lifetime. Using exacting scientific parameters, such as verifying birthmarks and scars and setting up double blinds, he found some pretty convincing evidence. For example, he interviewed a young boy who lived in a small village on one side of India. Few people in that village had ever journeyed much beyond it and none, they all maintained, had ever been to another village on the other side of the subcontinent. Yet this boy could recount with great accuracy the interior of the house in that village that he said he had lived in during his previous life. He described the family living there in great detail, including his former wife. He told the story of how he had died.

Stephenson then visited that village with the boy and found it precisely as the lad had described. The boy identified all of the family members—though one "brother" pretended to be another to test him. He wasn't fooled. His former wife, now remarried, burst into tears and hugged him. The entire family confirmed how he had died—in the rather unusual manner the boy had already described.

Okay, if we stretch we can come up with alternative explanations—such as that the villagers were having fun mucking about with the investigator or even that the boy had the capacity to remotely view that house across India. Notice that the explanations begin to sound more implausible than Stephenson's contention that human beings might live more than a single life. If this were his only example, that is one thing, but his research turned up hundreds of such examples. He discovered that children between the ages of three and five were especially likely to recall a former life with astonishing detail.[33]

---

33   Stephenson, I., *Twenty Cases Suggestive of Reincarnation* (1980); *Children Who Remember Previous Lives* (2000).

The Follow-Up Experience That Terrified Me

Over a decade later I walked into my favorite watering hole in Nevada City to get a beer after a long work day. I sat down at the bar beside an older man I'd never seen before but who seemed somehow familiar. He said something to me in the din of the bar that sounded like "vote." I took a pull on my beer and focused on the Giants' game on the TV, hoping to avoid a political discussion.

"You don't know what I'm talking about, do you?" he persisted.

I looked at him more closely. He had piercing blue eyes and very clean white hair combed straight back. He was wearing Levis and a dark blue flannel shirt. I guessed he was in his late 60s. He seemed sane and sober.

"I couldn't hear you before," I admitted.

"You're the one I sold the *boat* to," he said.

Not vote, *boat*. Since I'd never owned a boat in this life, I was puzzled.

"What boat are you talking about?" I asked.

"The one I sold to you in Sweden in 1286," he said, as matter-of-fact as if we were discussing the Giants' lack of run production.

I felt a chill run down my back at that moment. I was the only one who knew about my former experience in my therapy session. I hadn't even talked about it with my therapist. How could this man know about that?

"Oh," I laughed. "The one I got stuck in the ice? Freezing myself and my whole crew?"

"You wouldn't have gotten stuck in the ice," he said, shaking his head with authority. "You were too smart."

I was so shocked by the many implications of this brief conversation that, I blush to admit, I quickly finished my beer and fled. It was just too overwhelming for me to consider that not only might my "past life recall" have been spot on but that I was re-meeting someone I had known in that life. This possibility so upset the conventional boundaries of what reality might be that I was completely unnerved.

Please believe me when I say that, except for that first sip of beer, I was sober as a judge.

After sleeping on it, I kicked myself for not taking the conversation deeper. I went back to that bar every day for a week and looked all around town, but I never found the man again. I tried to tell myself that it had simply been a coincidence. But when I started computing the odds on that, I had to admit they were pretty slim. I still kick myself for my cowardice in fleeing, though when I examine the situation in retrospect, I realize that if some part of me hadn't known that I was facing something I sensed was true I wouldn't have been so frightened. I was scared precisely because my prior map wasn't fitting the territory.

Exploring Together

I tell you this story not to reveal what a scaredy-cat I was on that day but to encourage you to consider the possibility that there might be more to life than is dreamt of in our philosophies. As we explore Inner Space together, Yashi and I discover surprising new worlds and grow much closer. We have had some amazing experiences. Since we don't do drugs, these have all been while we are completely sober.

The same is likely to happen for you, with your partner. Like us, you can get there by trading feeling sessions, by sharing dreams, by going on drum journeys, or by entering the world of what Jung called "the active imagination."

Some people like to travel together to visit new countries and speak different languages. (If you and your partner find that brings you closer, by all means travel.) Having done extensive exploration of the outer world as a young man, I find myself much more interested in the inner one now. Besides, airplane seats are getting smaller and harder.

Such exploration may require you to suspend disbelief. If the idea that you're about to enter a past life scares you, reframe the exploration as imaginary. What Jung called "the active imagination" can be a very rich source of mutual exploration.

What follows is a shorter form of a set of instructions that I received, apparently by accident, in the mail many years ago that will help you explore what might be past life experiences. Yashi and I have found them helpful in opening the doors of perception into some fascinating and thought-provoking inner states. I pass them on to you in the event you and your partner might wish to explore this aspect of Inner Space together.

In any of these activities, what is most important is the experience itself. Our minds like to label things, to find a convenient pigeon-hole in which to file them away. We are uncomfortable with new experiences that challenge our world-views, as I was in the bar. I suggest that you restrain your mind from leaping to conclusions, from needing to label what you are experiencing before you have experienced it fully.

An explorer knows that she will be scared or uncomfortable at times and accepts those feelings as a part of the quest, well worth it because of the exciting discoveries to be made. There is no exploration that I know of that will yield such rich treasures as those to be found in Inner Space.

With the following exercise, as with a feeling session, I suggest that you create a "sacred space" that you consciously mark off from workaday reality by making a mutual appointment for it, by forestalling any interruptions, and by darkening the room. The Explorer removes his shoes and lies down on his back on a bed or mat on the floor and begins by focusing on the breath. The Guide then prepares the Explorer by clasping his legs, one at a time, just above the knee and massaging downwards, stopping briefly at the knee to make sure it is relaxed, then rubbing on down the shin, ankle, and foot. Massage the toes briefly and vigorously. Repeat this process quickly. Next, place the palm of your hand on the Explorer's forehead and, with a little pressure, move the skin of the forehead up and down, and then sideways for a few seconds. The Guide can then read through the following instructions for an exercise we might call "Time Travel":

Time Travel: Close your eyes and let yourself breathe deeply. (Pause) Become a few inches taller by allowing yourself to stretch out through the bottom of your feet. Tell me when you have done this. (Wait for him to confirm that he has accomplished this and pause for a few beats.) Go back to your normal size and tell me when you have done so. (Pause until you receive confirmation.)

This time, become a foot taller, and tell me when you've done this. (Wait for confirmation and pause for a few beats.) Return to your normal size. (Pause)

Now go to the other end of your body and become a few inches taller by extending yourself out through the top of your head. Tell me when you've done this. (Pause) Return to normal size. Tell me when you've done so. Good. Now become a foot taller through the top of your head. (Always ask him to tell you when he has accomplished the instruction.)

This time, extend yourself through the head, face, body, arms, legs, and feet. In other words, just blow yourself up like a balloon. Tell me as soon as you've done this. (Pause) Now go back to normal size.

Blow yourself up like a balloon again, only much larger this time. (Pause for his confirmation that he has done so.) Go quickly and stand in front of the building where you live. (As soon as he has done so, start him talking. Ask him to describe what he sees. If necessary, tell him what to look for, one at a time: Door, doorknob, windows, walkways, trees, shrubs, etc. After he has done so say—)

Go quickly and stand on the roof of the building and look down into the yard in font. What do you see? (Pause for this description.) Now, go about 500 feet up in the air and look down. What do you see?

At this point some people may get a little fearful, but remind him quickly that he is still safe in the room. Throughout his exercise, be jovial and keep your voice firm and convincing, yet ready to laugh. Keep the Explorer moving quickly and smoothly. If the Explorer protests that he is "imagining things" remind him gently that that is the purpose of this exercise in awareness and continue.

Is it daytime or nighttime? What makes you think so? (If it is nighttime or twilight in his vision, ask him to make it daylight—bright and sunny. If it is daytime, ask him to make it night. Have him change one to the other three times, but finish on a bright, sunny day.)

Who is making it night and day?

Most people will answer, "I am!" right away. However, if he hesitates for more than ten seconds ask him, "Are **you** making it night and day?" He will agree. It is very important that he understands the he is causing the change.

Are you still high in the air? Please keep the scene very bright. Come back to earth in another lifetime that you lived many years ago. Come down quickly as you go back in time. Bring your feet down quickly and firmly, but gently, and stand on the ground. Tell me as soon as you are there.

Watch the Explorer's face. As soon as there is eye movement under the lids tell him:

Please look down at your feet and tell me what you are wearing on them, if anything. What are you wearing on the lower part of your body? Look out through your eyes and listen through your ears. What do you see? Hear?

Wait for descriptions but keep the Explorer talking. Keep asking questions, moving forward in a roughly chronological order. You can also ask him to walk around and report what he encounters. When he's explored where he is, move him ahead in time: Skip a day, a week, a month or a year in his lifetime, but keep him moving and talking. At the end of the lifetime, ask the Explorer to go to an earlier lifetime by asking:

Come down in an earlier lifetime. Look down at your feet and tell me what you are wearing on them.

At the end of the second or third lifetime you have run through, ask the Explorer to "die" and follow through on the "death," asking:

What happens next? (You might need to ask this several times to elicit his full experience.)

When he has run incidents between his lives, tell him:

Go back and find your present parents, from the first time you saw them until after you were born.

When you discontinue the process at any time, ask the Explorer, "Do you see any need to continue at this time?" Let him or her decide when to stop.

Sharing Your Experiences

When you are present as the Explorer makes such forays into Inner Space, you will hear much about his or her experience as it unfolds. Afterwards, the Explorer will probably want to tell you more about the journey and its implications for this life. As with dreams, I suggest that as you hear about the inner experience you adopt the role of the good Listener rather than trying to interpret the experience. Give the Explorer the respect of allowing him or her to come to his or her own conclusions, which will occur, sooner or later.

There is a big part of any of us that wants to know what an inner experience "means," especially when it is numinous and mysterious. Sometimes you will know without question what the experience means to you. Other times you will have the slight anxiety of not-knowing for a time. At that point we are vulnerable to someone else's interpretation, which can at least give us an "answer" that will mitigate the anxiety. The problem is that when I hear your dream, past life, or other inner experience, I will project onto it my *own* movie, which will be different from yours. If you take it on as yours, it may relieve your anxiety temporarily but it will lead you away from your own truth.

My suggestion is that you develop your capacity to tolerate the anxiety of not-knowing and allow your own understanding to emerge with time. If you have questions about your experience, return to parts of it as you would a dream and open a dialog with those parts. For example, I might dialog with the encircling ice and tell it how frightened I am that it will immobilize the ship and freeze us all. Or I can ask my helmsman what help he needs to turn the ship about.

If the Explorer wishes for your insights, she will ask. I suggest that the Listener ask back, first, "Are you sure you want my projections on your experience?" If you get the green light you can then begin by saying, "Well, if this were *my* dream/ time travel," to remind yourself and the traveler that you're both entering the area of *your* psyche, not his or hers.

Then say what you're curious about. For instance, "I'd want to ask the crew to get out the oars and row us southward."

When done with this kind of mutual respect, a partner's perspective can help you go deeper into your personal experience.

Subsequent Sessions

When you do a second session, make the Explorer comfortable (but no need to massage) and tell him to turn the lights on inside. Then go quickly to where you left off last time.

Practice is essential. Soon an entire lifetime can be seen in a few minutes with all the senses giving information.

After you have "travelled" with a Guide half a dozen times, you will be able to do the process on your own, if you so choose. The advantages of doing so are that you can travel whenever you wish and that, by going solo, you may uncover material you are at first shy about sharing with your partner. In time, this shyness will pass.

The advantages of doing the process with your partner are that you will enjoy learning what your partner experiences as she experiences it, you will understand each other better and develop more and more compassion for each other, which will strengthen your connection. Since the primary purpose of this book is to help you build a strong relationship, I encourage you to share the experience as often as you like.

As you travel together into each other's active imagination (or is it really that you are seeing a reality?), you will find that you connect at what we might call a spiritual level. You might discover that some of what seem to be your past lives have overlapped—in ways that will give you great insight into your present interactions. The implications of what you discover will necessarily lead you into exciting discussions about the nature of reality and your place together in it. You might lose your fear of death. You might begin to suspect that the universe is out to do you good.

Is this real? Or just my imagination?

Many, if not most, people want to know whether what they've been experiencing on such a journey is "real." That is a normal human response—we have a metaphysical need for a meaningful cosmos. We'd like to understand the reality of our universe. That drive in us leads to some remarkable scientific discoveries and gives us the tantalizing hope that we'll be able to unravel the Great Mystery.

After a lifetime of trying to do so myself, I have come to the conclusion that the Great Mystery is aptly named. I don't think we're going to have conclusive scientific answers to some of the most fundamental questions about the basic nature of our reality.

We don't like that much—we have a primal dislike for ambiguity. Yet, as Jung pointed out, the capacity to tolerate ambiguity is a mark of maturity. Ultimately, at least while we are navigating this exciting and challenging Earthwalk, we're not going to *know*, at least cognitively, what the Great Mystery is all about.

Because we dislike not knowing, human beings turn to religion: How pleasant to know that the universe was created by Grandmother Spider or God or the Great Spaghetti Monster. How reassuring to believe that we will, if we have been "good," go on to a happy afterlife, perhaps involving wings and a harp or forty-four dewy-eyed virgins.

Unfortunately for the True Believer, there is no way to prove the reality or unreality of any of these lovely stories, although the True Believer will insist that his belief is absolutely true and will, historically, tend to kill anyone who doesn't agree with him. One must wonder why, if I truly believe in such a reality, I would need to slaughter those who are skeptical—unless I feared they might be right.

True Believers aside, the rest of us will need to deal with ambiguity about the nature of a Reality we won't be able to prove scientifically. You will probably have this experience as you explore what we call "past lives."

Having had many such experiences, my leaning at this time is toward the belief that we do in fact live many lives, but I do not need to convince anyone else of that—nor do I need to behead them if they disagree with me. Accepting that my reality has expanded through those experiences and that my relationship is richer for it is enough for me. I am coming to gain the capacity to tolerate ambiguity.

Scott Peck points out that when we have the choice between anchoring ourselves in a drab reality ("I only live once and then disappear.") or in a dramatic one ("I get to live many lives!"), why not pick the more exciting one?[34] It will make our lives a lot more fun.

Meanwhile, the Universe goes on, in all its magnificent Reality. Ain't it great?

---

34 *The Road Less Traveled*, (1988).

What If Scary Feelings Come Up?

As you make these exploratory journeys, most of the time you'll have pleasant and enjoyable trips. Occasionally, you might be bored. And sometimes you might get frightened.

Any explorer, venturing out onto the blank parts of her map, will encounter experiences that are unfamiliar. A natural human reaction to the unfamiliar is fear. When fear comes up, don't avoid it. The way out is through. Breathe more deeply, and on each exhale scream into the fear. Scream "I'm scared!" or just make sounds. Ride the wave of the feeling, as if you were riding a boogie board at the beach, as far as you can go that day.

Fear is a challenging feeling to feel alone. It really helps to have your partner or a buddy there with you to ground you with their presence.

Here's what I can assure you after guiding hundreds of people through such scary places: If you are not a schizophrenic and you aren't using drugs as booster rockets, *any* feeling that comes up will pass in time. Feelings are transitory. There is a very conservative gating mechanism in the hippocampus that lifts only enough to give us experiences that we can reasonably handle. You can count on it to close the gate before you get too freaked out. However, many drugs, including modern marijuana, LSD, and ecstasy, can blow the hinges off this gate and we can be flooded with feelings and images that can lead to a psychotic break. I recommend not using any substance while you are making these journeys. You don't need them to explore Inner Space.

In fact, absolutely sober explorations can take you to amazing and sometimes scary places.

I'll give you an example of what you might run in to as you go deeper into your explorations through a world-changing experience I had early in primal therapy.

Primal therapy begins with what is called The Intensive, which is a three-week period during which you do nothing but therapy every day. Literally nothing: You don't read or watch TV or talk on the phone or operate a computer. You don't meditate or masturbate or exercise. You check into a bare room, unplug the phone and TV, and stare at the bare wall for 24 hours before your first session. After your session, you get something to eat, then go back to your room until the next day's session.

The isolation and reduction of exterior stimulae allow your feelings to come up into your attention. As they do so, you realize *that most of what most people spend most of their lives doing is creating distractions from what they are really feeling.*

The sessions themselves entail minimal talk and maximum feeling. You come into a semi-darkened room where your therapist is waiting for you. No pleasantries. You lie down on a mat, close your eyes, and breathe deeply. As soon as a feeling comes up, which will happen fairly quickly when nothing else is in the way, you express it in sounds.

During the first week I spent a lot of time screaming in rage and pounding the mat. I was angry at my current life situation and, beneath that, with a father who had been critical and distant.

Early in the second week I found very powerful feelings coming up. At first I raged, but then I found my body leading me. Without knowing why, I pushed with my feet until my body scooted up the mat and the top of my head squished into the pillow that was against the wall. At that point my body arched up into a half circle and my voice changed to the high keening of an infant's wail.

That totally freaked me out. I had no idea what was going on. Was I possessed? It felt like what I'd imagined a demonic possession to be like. I was so scared that my process shut down.

"What am I doing?" I asked David Mills, my therapist.

"Just stay with the feelings," David said. David had absolute faith in the feeling process.

It took a while for me to return to where I'd been. Same stuff: Feet thrusting, body arching, head driving into the pillow, weird sounds emanating from my mouth that I couldn't believe I was capable of making.

My God! I thought, *I'm getting born!*

I couldn't stop my frightened mind from trying to make sense of what I was experiencing. Once again my mind jerked me out of the process. I lay on the mat panting, my mind reeling. I had no inkling of the possibility that anyone (this was 1973) could re-experience their birth. I'd never even heard of such a thing. I bought into the then-current belief that neonates and even infants can't remember anything from much before two years old.

I did know that though the early psychoanalytic movement had hypothesized that the "birth trauma" was the root of all human anxiety, most of Freud's circle didn't think anyone retained a clear memory of birth. Certainly most of the doctors I knew in 1973 would have laughed themselves giddy at such a notion.

Even David had never witnessed it. He called in his supervisor, Mark, to the next session and afterwards they conferred. When I tried to get Mark to tell me what was going on, he wisely refused.

"Just go with what you're experiencing. Don't try to pigeonhole it. It will become clear as you go with it."

So I went with the feelings and movements and weird sounds and, over the course of a couple weeks, I re-lived my entire birth, from leaving the womb to moving down the vaginal canal to being shoulder-stuck with my head out, where I could see bright lights and the half-faces of masked human figures in white coats who were just standing there witnessing my distress. With a Herculean effort that involved a massive rage alternating with a paralyzing terror, I finally managed to fight myself free.

Even when I was experiencing this profound passage, a skeptical part of my mind kept insisting that I couldn't possibly be doing so, since we all know that's impossible. In the end, however, as my actual experience overwhelmed my prior beliefs, I had to admit to myself that the skeptical part of me was prejudiced and quite unscientific. But I know, from that dialectic inside me, how challenging it will be for anyone to have an open mind on this topic—and many others. When you've been brought up to see a flat earth it's really tough to imagine that it's round, even when you can see that a ship's hull disappears over the horizon while the masts are still visible.

Having relived my birth, my mind was flooded with connections between what I had gone through on that day and the shape of the rest of my life.

"My God," I said to David, "no wonder I've always panicked and then fought like a cornered rat when I've felt stuck in any way. No wonder that I've never liked going into hospitals. No wonder I've been so angry all my life."

The connections between how I had been born and my personality kept coming. I "got," for instance, the origins of my strong belief that I had to accomplish everything on my own and that it was futile to ask for help. Most importantly, however, I was freed from most such powerful imprints. Today, I can ask for help, I can go into hospitals (though I'm never entirely comfortable in them), and I carry very little archaic anger around with me. But one word of advice: Don't push me into a tight corner.

Of my birth I had previously known only that I had been the very first "natural" birth at New Haven General. My grandfather Ide, bless him, had searched around to find an obstetrician who would consent to a birth without the "benefits" of drugs or forceps. My mother and father bravely agreed to what was at the time a radical concept—allowing a birth to happen as it had for humans for millions of years.

A few months after I had re-experienced my birth in therapy, I gave my mother a phone call and asked her about her memory.

"Mom," I asked, "did my head come out pretty easily and then my shoulders get stuck for a long time?"

There was a silence on the telephone line.

"Are you still there?" I asked.

"How did you know that?" Mom countered. "I never told you about that."

"I've been reliving it."

My mother didn't even question that I could. She'd always trusted my perceptions.

"Your shoulders were stuck for an hour," she said. "Your birth had gone very easily up till then."

"Were there a lot of people in white coats and masks standing around doing nothing?"

"Most of the hospital staff had come in to watch," she said. "They'd never witnessed a natural birth before."

"How was the birth for you?" I asked.

"It hurt like the dickens when your shoulders got stuck. I could feel you kicking like a mule. I wished one of those professionals had been able to do something to help. I assumed 'natural birth' meant I had to do it all on my own. I got through it by quoting Byron to myself."

"Yeah," I said, "I felt out of connection with you at that point. And I've never liked Byron."

I corroborated a few other details with her before we finished our conversation. While I felt good that our recall of our mutual experience matched, I hadn't needed that to know, absolutely, that my own recall was accurate, for me.

When my first son was to be born, at home, I told our midwife about being shoulder-stuck at my own birth. She said that birth patterns often repeat in families and that it wouldn't be a problem. Sure enough, Nate experienced the same hang-up. However, it took the midwife only a nanosecond to skillfully and gently pull one and then the other shoulder free.

Having had this experience, Nate has become a journalist who writes about birth and the interface of the natural and the technological. He won an award for his expose of the fact that the rate of maternal deaths in hospitals has *tripled* in California over the last ten years. His book on the question "Is natural good?"—entitled *All Natural*—was released by Rodale Press on January 29, 2013. The first chapter is on birth. It's a heck of a book.

Many of the clients I have worked with in primal therapy have relived their own births—and even neonatal experiences. They retrieve remarkable information and understanding of their present lives by doing so. More importantly, they free themselves of old, dysfunctional patterns of behavior.

A man who had a Caesarean birth said he realized why he had always felt that he had to rely on others to get him through difficult times and that any effort on his part wouldn't be effective. His partners were usually frustrated with the fact that he seemed excessively "laid back" and distant. They felt like they had to step in and do things for him. For example, he'd often forget his hat or coat—at a concert, in a restaurant—and his partner would have to pick it up for him.

One woman, who was always fearful that her partners in relationship would restrict her and suffocate her, re-experienced the fact that she had had a twin who had died in the womb. She had to feel the immense guilt that she had "killed" her twin by being the one to survive on the meager resources available. She realized that once she moved in with a partner, the old "only one of us can survive" feelings were reactivated.

While the understanding that comes from reliving birth and other early experiences is wonderful, what is more important is that the person who can go through such feelings can then be free of their hold on him or her. For example, the Caesarean-birthed man was able to avoid the old paralysis and to take care of himself in the present rather than rely upon a partner to do for him. The untwinned woman is now in a thriving relationship.

You can see that if one partner is stuck in one of these feelings, such as "Only one of us can survive here" or "I have to rely on you to do for me" or "Don't fence me in!" that they and their partners will have big challenges. Furthermore, there is no cognitive solution to such issues. You can attempt to construct all manner of work-arounds to these primal imprints but any purely cognitive approach will ultimately fail. The only way out of them is, like birth, *through* the difficult feelings. The neocortex is powerless to solve issues that reside in the brain stem. You have to access the reptile brain directly—or is such information held in the very cells of our bodies, as Dr. Graham Farrant believed?[35]

Wherever such information resides in us, you might find it coming through when you are making your explorations of Inner Space. When it does, accept and ride with it as much as you can: It will take you to places that challenge our received ideas of who we are and what the Great Mystery is all about. These experiences will stretch your understanding of what we call the spiritual, to which we will turn next. They will also form deep connections between you and your partner.

If what comes to you is too scary for you to deal with by yourself, you can hire a feeling-based therapist as a guide. Best is someone who's already been there. At the very least you want to find a therapist who doesn't believe you are crazy to be having birth feelings or experiencing a past life.

---

35   See, e.g., "Cellular Consciousness and Conception," *Pre- & Perinatal Psychology News*, vol. 2, issue 2 (summer), 1988.

Conclusion

Through such practices as mindfulness, feeling sessions, dreamwork, drum journeys, and past life exploration, you and your partner can, if you wish, explore a wider reality than most people know or even imagine. In so doing you will build a much deeper intimacy than is available to those whose whole reality is mediated mostly by toil and television. You will get to know yourselves and each other at much deeper and more deeply connecting levels. On your explorations of Inner Space, you will encounter experiences that will show you glimpses of alternative realities—of what I have been calling the Spirit World. It is to that world that we will turn next.

I wish you much excitement and wonder as you color in many of the blank spaces on your maps together.

CHAPTER 7:
RELATIONSHIP AS A
SPIRITUAL PRACTICE

No man is an island entire of itself; every man
is a piece of the continent, a part of the main;
if a clod be washed away by the sea, Europe
is the less, as well as if a promontory were, as
well as a manor of thy friends or of thine
own were; any man's death diminishes me,
because I am involved in mankind.
And therefore never send to know for whom
the bell tolls; it tolls for thee.
—John Donne

A continuing theme throughout both this book and *Real Relationship* has been that our relationships pull us toward spiritual development as magnets pull iron filings. I want to address that idea in more detail in this last chapter, to give you a larger vision of your relationship and what it might mean for you. And, although you might have noticed that I have some problems with some parts of organized religion, please don't take that to mean that I discourage you from participating in the religion of your choice. In fact, I encourage it. There is much evidence that a couple who share a spiritual perspective are more likely to endure. If your spiritual practice is already in place and working for you, great. Please read the following information with the understanding that I have no need to proselytize or convince you of any different perspective. I hope what follows will only enrich your current spiritual practice and help you deepen your connection with your partner.

In *Real Relationship* I discussed avoiding those big, general words, called "nominalisms" by philosophers (which is just a fancy way of saying "name-words") because they mean very different things to different people. Well, "spiritual" is just such a word. In fact, words such as *spiritual, religion, God*, and *faith* are probably among the most diluted words in use. When I use the word "God" do you see an old man with a long white beard? A burning bush?[36]

Or, like many of our most thoughtful scientists, do you think of the mysterious forces of the larger Universe?

What is tragic, of course, is that people have killed and died and will continue to kill and die because their name for that force is a bit different from someone else's. Today Shia and Sunni blow one another to bits. Not so long ago, Protestant and Catholic blew each other to bits.

There can be a similar dogmatism around the word "spiritual."

I would like to use the word not as a hard definition but as a signpost that points you in a general direction and which you are free to fill in with your own beliefs, values, and wisdom. In the general direction of that which brings

---

36 One year as our *Contacting Mother Earth*™ group was hiking into Sacred Lake, we found that a small pine near the lake was ablaze, having caught fire through its roots from a nearby (and illegal) fire pit that someone had thought he'd put dead out. We dropped our packs, dug out the underground fire, carried water from the lake, and eventually extinguished the fire. My elder son, Nate, upon hearing of this, raised an eyebrow. "Are you telling me," he said, "that while on a vision quest you came upon a burning bush and dowsed it out with water? Did you at least *try* to converse with it first?"

out the best in you—what Abe Maslow would call your *self-actualization*. What helps you become the best possible human being you can be? And, at the same time, what helps you realize and manifest your connection to our planet and to the larger Cosmos? One of the primary vehicles most of us have for such achievements is our relationships: First, our relationship with ourselves, especially the unconscious parts of ourselves. Second, our relationship with our partners. Third, our relationship with Mother Earth. And, fourth, our relationship with the Cosmos or what the Lakota would call Wakan Tanka, which might be translated as "The Great Mystery." Other signposts for that are God or Allah or Yaweh.

I think we need to include the reality of these larger perspectives of our relation to the Earth and to the Cosmos. The personal and the interpersonal occur not in a vacuum but within the context of what we might call the *circa-personal*: That which surrounds, flows through, and embraces us. We are the children of a vast universe. Until we envision ourselves in the larger reality of that universe, we are like children attempting to play Solitaire with a third of a deck of cards. We are unmoored, adrift upon a sea of night. We need to feel we are not *on* this planet but *of* her. That we do not spin *in* this universe but as an integral part of its vast web.

So long as we have this misconception that we are somehow separate from our Earth and our universe, we will feel lonely and fearful. *We will then attempt to use our relationships to palliate our loneliness rather than to grow our connection to the larger reality.*

I came to this understanding not so much through thought as through intuition, an intuition that any psychology or relationship constrained by four walls or an urban consciousness lacked important chunks of reality. I think this perspective is an important one if we are to have either inner serenity or truly loving relationships.

But already I am becoming too general. I would like to make this concept more specific and real by telling you a piece of my own story of how I came to this broader conception of Spirit. How you come to Spirit will be an individual journey. "Each man enters the wilderness of the Spirit at that point that he feels is best, where there is no path," sings the harper of the story of the Quest for the Grail. I tell you the following tale not to suggest that you should make a similar quest, but to give you a more specific idea of that broader concept we call the "spiritual."

One Person's Opening to a Larger Vision

One point to mark where it began might be the three weeks of solitude that I endured during the Intensive portion of my primal therapy, which I mentioned in the last chapter. That sacred space of profound self-care and deep exploration of my unconscious was so important in opening my spirituality that afterwards I made a vow to take a renewing week of solitude every year. When it came time to take that week for myself, however, the idea of doing so in the kind of four-walled cubicle where I'd done my Intensive was unattractive. Instead, I decided to go backpacking alone among the alpine lakes, glacier-worn granite, and delicate wildflowers of the High Sierra. I began my walkabout from the beauty of Tuolumne Meadows and soon left the trail and ascended into the surrounding mountains. Being alone in the wilderness caused me only a mild concern until the sun started to slip behind the peaks to the west.

I had seen no people since before noon. I was five miles of rugged cross-country bushwhacking from the nearest trail. Striking out into the deep wild had ratcheted up my fears a tad—what if I broke an ankle? But I knew intuitively that what my soul craved was solitude in Nature. Although I'd probably heard of how Native Americans made their vision quests, I wasn't making a formal quest—I was just following an inner guidance.

I'd reached the secluded lake that had looked so alluring on my map. As the sunset's pinks and purples were reflected in the mirror of the darkening water, I put together my fishing pole, cast my line out twice, and hauled in two fat trout for dinner. As they sizzled in my fry pan, smelling delicious, I thought, *Hmm. If there are any bears around here, they're gonna smell this, too.* When I looked up, sure enough, there was a big black bear, not twenty yards away, staring at me with beady eyes and twitching nostrils.

Without fanfare, he charged.

Although I'd often seen black bears before, I'd never been charged by one. They seldom are so aggressive. Having a quarter ton of frothing fury hurtling toward me definitely stopped my world. In that moment I lost all civilized thought process. I regressed to Neanderthal man.

Transferring the precious pan of trout to my left hand, I picked up in my right a stone so big that I doubt I could have budged it with both hands in a normal state of consciousness.

The bear was coming straight at me, ten yards away now,

and I—or my inner caveman—bellowed a primal scream and hurled the stone. As I did so, the bear veered away and was passing by when my forebrain clicked back on and began shrieking hysterically: *You idiot! He was leaving! Now he's going to be really pissed off!*

The stone, hurled with a strength far beyond my normal one, caught the bear, who was then probably five yards away, right over the heart. I would not have been surprised had he dropped dead—or turned to maul me. I heard a deep *Thunk!* such as when you strike a hollow log.

The bear didn't even break stride. Running like a fullback, he disappeared into the firs.

I had a post-traumatic stress reaction, shaking violently from head to toe. I put the frying pan down lest I spill the priceless trout. I sobbed as the shadows lengthened.

When I could function again, I gobbled the trout and then gathered a head-high pile of firewood. With shaking hands I managed to strike a match to build a bonfire. Pumped with adrenaline, I tended my fire like some ancient Druid through the slow wheeling of the stars. I sharpened one end of a stout eight-foot fir branch and fire-hardened the point. I was sure the bear would return in the night for his vengeance. Sleep was out of the question.

The bear did not come back that night. I had to admit that revenge was my own human projection. When the rosy fingers of dawn finally began poking up into the east, I found myself singing and dancing with joy. As I lifted up my arms and sang up the rising red orb, I understood why nature peoples have worshipped Father Sun. I had been delivered from the terrifying dragons of night.

Much later, as I was studying the shamanic world view, I

learned that Brother Bear is the guide to the Looks-Within-Place: To Inner Space. He is the Guardian of the West. My bear had charged me with the sunset at his back. And, boy, did he ever open me up to examining my inner world.

I left that lake, crossed a rich green valley, and climbed a rockface that I hoped no bear could ascend. Atop the ridge I could look back to where I'd endured the night before and see the stand of firs around what I called Hungry Bear Lake. The sky was a robin's egg blue, with soft lacings of cloud. I was all alone, deep in the wilderness, with no protection other than my wits and my Neanderthal collective unconsciousness. Suddenly, I realized that that was enough, that I was enough. I knew that, barring a catastrophic accident, I could survive in Nature.

It was as if a great burden fell away from me, and I wept. Wept for all the unnecessary fear that I'd carried all my life. Wept at how I'd been afraid to trust my Mother's bounty. She was all around me now, gently cradling me. The granite cliffs were her strong arms, the grass and trees her hair, the lakes the milk of her breasts.

Below me lay a lovely oval lake surrounded by soft duff and an impressionist's pastel of wildflowers. As I looked down at the lake, a huge bear, cinnamon-colored, emerged from the forest at its western end and slowly ambled around its shore.

I felt no fear. Bears were no longer my foe but my special relations. I *knew* they would not hurt me, if I respected the rules of Nature. Nature was now family to me.

Since that day, I have made a yearly pilgrimage to that visionary lake, which I call Sacred Lake, to renew my sense of oneness with Mother Nature and all her children. Usually the bears, who I have come to know personally, try to steal my food. Usually I shout them off before they do so. It's a game we play, more exciting and real than most. When Bear graces me with such a visitation, to play with me, the hair always stands up on the back of my neck and I experience for a time the awe and sublimity that Man has felt in untamed Nature for millennia, and I know a deep aliveness.

Sharing the Opportunity with Others

Soon after this experience, it came to me that I could share this opportunity with others. I now knew that there were available in Nature experiences that people would not have in my consulting room. I began taking a small tribe of people (a different one each year) out of the city into the wilderness to open to them the opportunities presented by an experience of Nature wherein they might lose some of their fears and discover a nurturing mother who embraced them lovingly. I called this experience *Contacting Mother Earth*™.

I have been leading (and more recently co-leading with Yashi) this wilderness experience for over four decades as of this writing. During that time it has evolved from a long weekend into a six day trip. On the first two days we hike into some sacred ground, doing a variety of exercises intended to help people open to their bodies and senses and to their tribe members. Then we scatter out around a lake basin for one or two days of fasting and solitude. When we re-gather we break the fast with fresh foods from our Mother (Yashi collects a salad of miner's lettuce, Mariposa lilies, and gooseberries) and share what we have experienced, if we choose.

(As in any of our experiences, members always have the right to pass on any given activity—a concept I suggest you incorporate into your relationship.) At the fast-breaking I try to provide enough freshly-caught trout to feed the tribe, commemorating both my experience at Hungry Bear Lake and an earlier one Christians will remember.

During this week together we engage in exercises designed to help break us out of our ego-shells and open us to reconnection with our deeper selves, our planet, and the Cosmos. Being no true believer, I have no dogma I need others to imbibe. I have only a perspective and a way of being to share. Yashi and I use Nature lore, storytelling, drumming, shamanic journeying, movement, poetry, dreamwork, group process, and whatever comes up to help create the doorway. Whether anyone wishes to go through is up to each individual.

We lead this quest each year as an augmentation to our indoor work as psychotherapists, for we realize the limitations of trying to help people grow and open when separated from their natural and cosmological environment. What we know is that people have great difficulty being fully human in four-walled rooms or concrete cities. We are children of this planet and these stars. We have artificially separated ourselves, to our sad loss, from the planet which bears us and the cosmos of which we are an integral part. Our pavements and streetlights and TVs and house walls cut us off from our Source. Self-exiled and imprisoned, we lose intimate connection with what is real.

People speak carelessly of the "real world" to mean the non-academic world of commerce, the courts, and war. But these are not the real world any more than academia is. Both are but human excrescences upon the face of the Real, like daubs of metallic paint upon a granite boulder or a towering redwood.

The Real World is rooted in our planet, born of our Cosmos. What is real is what was here before we evolved and what will remain long after we, at least in our present form, have gone the way of the dinosaur and the dodo.

We are but one of the many children Mother Nature has spawned. We are troubled if clever children, emotionally disturbed, given to bitter wrangling, and having the questionable distinction of being the only animal willing to risk the wholesale destruction of its own species—and even of the whole planet. We also have the potential for great love and kindness.

One possibility is to heal ourselves emotionally and learn to live in harmony with one another and our Mother. Our relationships present just such an opportunity for healing. Can we learn to live in relative harmony with one Other? But our Mother will survive whether we are naughty or nice. To ask what we can do about saving the Earth seems to me an incredible arrogance; the real question is what She will do about us.[37]

"The Earth is infected," wrote the visionary D.H. Lawrence, "with a disease called Man." Since Lawrence was no sexist, I assume by "Man" he meant "mankind" rather than testosterone poisoning.

Perhaps our Mother will have us cure this cancer with the radical radiation treatment we have created in our nuclear

---

37   I owe this lovely phrase to Theodore Rozak. See *Ecopsychology: Restoring the Earth, Healing the Mind* (1995). Ted graciously called me an ecopsychologist. In public.

weapons. Or perhaps we will be erased by some new virus she creates within us. While She is a forgiving mother, I don't think she will let us kill her and all her other children.

So whether we heal ourselves is of larger consequence than our individual happiness and our personal relationships. Our species hangs in the balance. And it is a planetary concern.

Relationship/Planet/Cosmos

Our relationships do not form in a vacuum, although we might have that illusion during the Romantic Stage ("We two against the world!"). Society impinges when a spouse is sent off to war or when a child is removed from a home by the legal system. Most of us these days feel the pressure of having to earn enough to survive, just to keep a roof over our heads and enough food on the table. As you know, couples today are re-negotiating roles, who works and how much, and how the children are cared for by whom. All of these societal issues affect our relationships profoundly.

I just began working with a couple whose relationship is being profoundly affected by his mother, who doesn't like his wife, and her ex-husband, who keeps suing her for the custody of their four-year old child. Much of their relationship stress is coming from both the legal system and people who were once dear to them.

Good therapists know something of these sociological factors and take them into consideration to help couples negotiate their way through this morass. Few therapists, however, know how important it might be to any relationship to be reconnected to Mother Earth and to the Cosmos. What we need is a larger, more spiritual perspective of how our relationship fits within these outer circles that surround us.

Up until the Industrial Revolution most people had this perspective, knowing "no Man is an Island," as John Donne so memorably phrased it. In Shakespeare's era, this perspective was called the Great Chain of Being. At the top were God and then the angels; toward the bottom were the lowliest worms. People were near the middle. Each creature was an important link of the chain.

If someone substituted a lover for the Great Mystery (as does Juliet when she says to Romeo, "Thou art the god of my idolatry"), every Elizabethan knew that such disruption of the Great Chain would bring tragedy. Love for another created being was all very well, so long as it did not forget its place in the larger Cosmos.

We have misplaced this sense of balance and proportion. We have lost the spiritual perspective, largely because we have witnessed our religions becoming purveyors of conflict, dogma, war, torture, prejudice, and abuse. Many contemporary religious organizations are hardly spiritual at all. Some are purveyors of hatred. Lacking wise spiritual guidance, we have lost our sense of our place in the Universe.

We are doomed to failure if we attempt to make our partner our spiritual pursuit. We need to find a spiritual core within ourselves from which we can then love our partner. "First a Self, then the possibility of a relationship."

Again, this is heady stuff. I want to try to ground it as specifically as I can.

The almost unconscious fears I had about being alone

in the wilderness, which were mediated more by childhood frights and Hollywood images than present reality, led my younger self to a mistrust of Nature, to treat her as something to fear, to armor myself against, and to conquer. Because I feared Her, I could not allow Her in deeply as a loving presence. Similarly in relationship: So long as I carried archaic fears based upon my old Pain and societal images, I had difficulty trusting a partner and I was protective of my vulnerabilities. It was only after I came to *know* that, no matter what feelings Nature or a relationship might kick up for me, I could be vulnerable and still take care of myself, that I was free to trust and to commit—to both a woman and to being fully present on this Earthwalk.

Trust resides, first of all, in knowing that I am a part of the Whole. So long as anyone believes he or she is separate, he or she will carry a deep, existential anxiety and feel alienated from the Whole. Trust also lives in being able to love fully and to know that I *will* be hurt—sometimes badly hurt—but that I can survive any hurt. Once I gain those capacities I am able to fully open and to expose my vulnerabilities to my partner. When I am fully open and vulnerable, I can truly love and be loved.

In this sense, love is letting go of fear. What do I have to fear, really, in the present? Abandonment, betrayal, ridicule, powerlessness, abuse? If the one I love hurts me in some way, *which will happen*, despite her best intentions, the real question is, "Do I have the capacity to experience that pain and to survive?"

Those who cannot answer with an unequivocal "Yes!" will of course be fearful of loving.

I am right to fear abandonment, for example, even in the

present, for it *will* occur. My Beloved will abandon me, as will yours. She abandons me when I need her to comfort me and she is unavailable. She abandons me when she is late. She might abandon me by dying first or by disappearing into Alzheimer's. There are countless ways in which we will be abandoned, against which it is impossible to erect effective defenses. Some abandonments are more painful than others. Given my own history of my mother "abandoning" me when my father came back from the war, what would be most painful for me would be to be replaced by another man. Especially one wearing a uniform.

And could I survive that? Having done my therapy and having learned how to enter and ride feelings back to their primal roots, having lived through countless small abandonments and a few big ones, I *know* that I could survive. I know that most of my fear is not actually present but past, and I know what that fear is and just how much it can hurt. Knowing all this through my feeling experience, I can be present and open with Love and my Beloved, in much the same way that I can now be present and open and safe in the wilderness.

The connection is, I think, that our fears of wilderness and the unconscious are analogous to our fears of relationship. We project our fears of the unexperienced experience in the unconscious onto both wilderness and relationship. The more adventurous among us might then seek them out, but as a challenge to be conquered rather than a Beloved to be trusted and cherished.

Rather than making sweet love to our Beloved and wilderness, many feel the need to conquer and rape them. The rape of the wilderness is obvious for all who have eyes to see.

The rape of relationship occurs around us every day. It happens every time any lover is fearful of accepting the Beloved as she is but attempts to change her into someone tamer. But she is a wild, natural being, with her bears and thunderstorms as well as her clear lakes and wildflowers. We do our Beloved great damage by attempting to transmogrify her into a suburban mall or a ticky-tacky housing development.

The irony is that if I do succeed in changing her from a stormy tempest into a tempest in a teapot I will no longer feel the same awesome love for her that I felt when she was a more organic, if less tame, part of the Cosmos.

As the hugely loving Aslan says in the Narnia books, "I am not a tame lion."

A central theme of this book (and *Real Relationship*) has been that love is letting someone else *be* rather than trying to change them. Learning to let go of our fears and our frantic struggles to control exterior reality—be it a person or a mountainside or the Cosmos—and to love them *as they are*, that is a great spiritual labor, perhaps the greatest. To do so, we must face our unconscious fears rather than attempting to work them out through micromanaging someone or something else. That is the core spiritual work that precedes and then continually accompanies good relationship.

Once I have done the bulk of that core work, the better half of my journey is complete. But not all. Any relationship, be it with Nature or a Beloved, will have terrifying tornadoes as well as days of heartbreaking beauty. Not being too much of a Fool, I don't run out naked into a thunderstorm. Lightning can kill. Being unprepared for a sudden snowfall in the tall mountains—even in August—is potentially lethal. Nor do I recommend kissing rattlesnakes.

Similarly with my Beloved. She is usually a warm summer's day, rich with lovely flowers and birdsong. I love her sunrise and sunset, the richness of her stars at night. It is easy to be completely open to these parts of her. But the sudden lightning of her rage or the venom of her tongue I take precautions around. Just as it is not trusting but stupid to swim while lightning flashes, it is unwise for me to proffer my heart when my Beloved is in a mood. In both cases, better to hunker down and watch the storm from a safe place, accepting and even enjoying it for what it is while not risking injury or death.

On Trust

There's a lot of confusion about trust. Most people seem to think it means expecting the best in all situations, as does the naïve lad Candide in Voltaire's great book of that name. They're then upset when their expectations aren't met. Do you remember the chapter on expectations in *Real Relationship*? It never hurts to re-read.

There's a cogent Chinese parable about a man who found a frozen snake on an icy winter's day. He took the snake home, warmed it by the fire, and gave it warm milk to drink from his favorite saucer. Once it warmed up and had drunk some milk, the snake bit him on the hand. As the deadly poison coursed through his veins, the man cried out, "Ungrateful snake! How could you do this to me?! I saved your life! I took you into my home! I warmed you at my hearth! I fed you sweet milk! And this is how you repay me?!"

The snake yawned and replied: "Don't blame me, buster.

You knew I was a snake when you picked me up."

Expecting a snake not to bite is not trusting but stupid. Biting is a part of its snaky nature. In fact, you can trust a snake to strike, a wolf to howl, and a salmon to swim upstream. A bear will try to steal your unprotected food. Being upset with any of them for doing what is natural to them is demented.

But we do this to the people we love all the time.

Recently a man came into my office, distraught that his lover was habitually late.

"What can I do about this flaw in her character?" he wondered.

I asked him how long he'd know her.

"Five years, and she's been late at least once a day the whole five years. She'll be late to her own funeral."

While knowing, absolutely, that being late was a part of who she was and had always been, he was unaccepting about this part of her that was inconvenient for him. He wanted me to tell him how to change her. Instead, I suggested that he trust her.

"To be on time??"

"No. To be late."

He looked at me as if I were crazy.

I pointed out that he *knew* she'd be chronically late. If that quality was too upsetting for him, he had the choice of leaving the relationship. If he chose to stay, he could trust her to be late and build that into his job description, figuring out ways to organize around it.

Similarly, we can trust Lucy to yank the football away every time Charlie Brown tries to kick it and we can trust politicians to break their campaign promises. Intelligent trust is based upon reality, not the way we'd like things to be.

Exercise: Make a list of the traits of a loved one that drive you up the wall. How many of these traits have you struggled to change? How much luck have you had doing so? What do you conclude?

Now, think about these traits of your loved one as simply parts of them, like a snake's fangs or a dog's fleas. Can you trust your loved one to have their traits?

Trusting them to be *as they are*, can you still love this person? How will *you* organize around these inconvenient traits that you can trust will be there so that they become less annoying for you?

Love is partly made up of acceptance, learning reality-based trust, and letting go of the fear that if we don't control the loved one they will hurt us. A goodly portion of our spiritual work is to release that fear and our attempts to control the realities around us. A continual spiritual task is to let your Beloved—and the Universe—be.

As we learn to let our Beloveds be, we will find that we can do so increasingly with ourselves, with others, and with our planet.

Cosmological Relationship

A relationship confined by four walls, a concrete patio, and a fence is cut off from the Earth and the Cosmos. Some people manage to keep a fichus or a housecat "alive" for years in a city apartment, though I wonder about the quality of that life. Similarly, a relationship that is cut off from the larger Cosmos is like a redwood trying to flourish in a hothouse. I imagine that sometimes it's done, but at great cost.

When I can let go of my fearfulness that attempts to change my Beloved from her wild nature into what might be safer and more convenient for me, I must then deal with her not as a sanitized, rubber blow-up doll but as an organic part of the Earth and the Universe. When I accept and love her as Wild Woman, as a flower conceived by Mother Earth, as a vivid star in the heavens, then I open myself to cosmological relationship.

The fearful perspective helps define us as two ant-beings whose existence is focused upon the angle of toilet seats and the accumulation and dispersing of little greenish pieces of paper. The loving perspective helps define us as two souls intertwining through our marvelous bodies and challenging, fascinating personalities as we come to know the Cosmos better through the quirky dance of our union.

One view is that we are two lumps of protoplasm that merge, perhaps engender other lumps, and dissolve back into the soil, having duly paid our requisite amount of income tax. Another is that we are two eternal parts of the Cosmos who will perhaps meet in many forms.

I suggest we choose the option that seems to be more interesting.

Once I step inside the cosmological perspective, I am in a place of wonder and excitement. Everything is imbued with significance. Everything glows with soul. This view—that everything that is, including our relationship, is Holy—is fundamental to the way a poet like William Blake or a shaman sees the Cosmos.

The Old Shaman Sings

On one of my quests, I met a shaman at Sacred Lake.

Imagine, if you will, that you are sitting with me beside my small fire of deadwood broken off from the surrounding trees. Millions of stars cast an eerie light over the face of the sheer granite wall that rises vertically behind the gently lapping waters of the lake. Occasionally the fiery trail of a meteor illuminates the sky, joining with the sparks of our fire that ascend toward heaven.

Suddenly, as though he had appeared from out of the earth, we see, sitting across the fire from us, a strange old man clad in the skins of animals—deer, beaver, bear, wolf. His hair is long and white and adorned with two eagle feathers. He wears a necklace of the claws of a bear. His eyes are closed and he is humming a melody in a minor key. One hand dips into an otter-skin pouch at his side and scatters sweet herbs onto the fire.

Do not flee. I know this shaman from my dreams. He is a wise man of great spiritual understanding.

The melody he hums grows louder now and we begin to make out what seem to be words in some outlandish language full of gutturals and glottal stops. Yet, was we listen more attentively, we can begin to understand:

In the beginning there was only the Great Mystery, and She was bored with being great, and so She conceived the Cosmic Game, which was to fragment herself into millions upon millions of parts, each of them Her, and not one of them knowing it was Her or that the Divine Dance was for all the fragments to separate, to dance in intricate steps, and then gradually reconnect once more in the One, if they could.

And so there was a blinding explosion of a magnitude unimaginable as She split into millions upon millions of fragments, some huge as suns, some tiny as grains of sand, and these parts hurtled away from one another, and not one of these parts knew or remembered that it was a part of the Great Mystery which lives in all things.

And so, my children, All that you see and taste and breathe on this night—you and I, this cool wind off the mountaintop, this pennyroyal tea we drink, this wall of granite and the countless stars beyond—All are but fragments of the Great One. To us it seems that stars and moon, you and I, lake and mountain are all separate, and so it is. And at the same time we are all connected, all One, for we are all parts of the Great Mystery which lives in each of us.

I know this, for it came to me in my Vision.

And now all of these seemingly separate pieces of the One are dancing across the great breast of sky as we have for countless eons, linked by that mysterious power of attraction called gravity or love that those with clever minds even now puzzle over and attempt to link as a Unified Force. What I know is that what we call "love" is the binding force of the Great One, as the parts of being are drawn together.

When we love, we join with another fragment of the Universe in such a way that for a time our illusion of separateness is dissolved and we experience the bliss of Oneness. If we feel that much bliss with but one other fragment, imagine how we will feel when we are all reconnected!

And when we experience such cosmic union, we are both blissful and frightened, for we are confused about what is All and what is "I," for that confusion is primordial from the first

Big Bang. It is difficult for us to grasp that we exist both as a separate "I" and unified Great One at the same moment. Naturally, for we have contradictory impulses within us—the desire to be separate that the Great Mystery manifested in the Big Bang and the desire to be One which is the ultimate "winning" of the Game.

Do not fret yourselves, my children. There is no hurry to achieve anything. Enjoy your separateness. Enjoy your eventual reunion. And after we are all One once again, there will be another Big Bang and the whole Game will begin again. It has happened countless times before and will happen countless times again, throughout all Eternity.

Right now, you are having the experience of separateness. Enjoy this part of the Game, for that illusion is very real at this moment. See! I am here and you are there, with this magic we call Fire between us. You hear me speak words you have not heard before, in a strange tongue, and this too is part of the Game, which one part of us relishes. Being separate, knowing what it is to be within the finite shell of a "human being" or a "rabbit" or a "star," that is something!

However, there can also be great pain in such separateness, for another and deeper part of us hungers for wholeness, to be One again. There is a greater pain in the belief that the Grand Illusion is the only reality when it is but one reality. The actual Reality, which all sages through time have spoken of, is that we are all One, that we are in fact the Great Mystery fragmented for a few billion moons.

And so, my children, when you have an experience of Oneness, be it with a special place, or a loving animal, or another two-legged, relish that. For in that experience of Oneness you taste the actual Oneness of the Great Mystery. Love leads us to taste that Oneness and will bring us home, over and again, through the vast ages, to our essential Oneness again.

But do not cling! Do not cling even to Oneness, for that in itself can be boring, or to Separateness, for that in itself can be frightening. The art of life is learning to shuttle, as the Great One does, back and forth between Oneness and Separateness, between the Inhalation and the Exhalation.

Loving relationships lend us the possibility of experiencing both Oneness and Separateness. When we fall in love, we feel at One. We make love and for a moment touch the Cosmos. Then our bodies disengage, and we think it would be pleasant to fall into separate sleep. The next morning we might argue over whether to hunt elk or dig up yampa. We do not see that these arguments are but devices to pull us from the Oneness toward greater Separateness. Once we are Separate, then we can reunite in greater Oneness. And so it goes.

Our error is that we attempt to cling to either Separateness or Oneness rather than accepting that both exist simultaneously.

Our blindness is that we forget that we are all One anyway and that this Separateness is but a Game for us to enjoy.

In relationship we can learn to play the Cosmic Game as the Great One does. We can take the long view, as does the Great One, and enjoy the Separateness as much as the Oneness, and we can enjoy the Dance as we move from one to the other and back again.

And so, my children, only listen within, to the Great Mystery that lives in you, that is you. Listen to when you wish Union and when you wish Separation. Of course one of you will sometimes wish Union when the other wishes Separateness, and that is only a device of the Divine Game. The art of *relationship is learning how to Dance together, from Separation to Oneness and back again. In this Dance, we mirror the Dance of the Great Mystery. Dance, my children, dance!*

We find ourselves startled, as if awaking abruptly from a dream, and trying to get our bearings. The Old Shaman has disappeared as suddenly and mysteriously as he came. The white cliff is still here, and the lake and the stars and the embers of the fire, though we see them now in a new way.

Relationship as a Spiritual Journey

By reframing our relationship as a spiritual journey that we are taking together on this Earthwalk (as the Old Shaman would call it), we open ourselves to a larger perspective that brings about a fundamental paradigm shift: From looking at our relationship as something out of which to squeeze comfort and security to a path with heart that will at times be challenging and difficult. More basically, from a *goal to be achieved* to an *ongoing process* that we (mostly) relish together.

Once when the Old Shaman and I were traveling across a high desert in an old rattletrap of a loaner car to reach a certain hot springs by nightfall for a marriage at which he was to officiate, the Old Shaman taught me something of releasing the goal and being in the process when we had a flat tire. I should mention that I did not have an intimate partner at the time. I managed to steer the wobbling car safely off the blacktop onto the sandy shoulder. Of course there was no spare anywhere that I could find in the trunk.

I was frustrated that we were now marooned in an inhospitable place and would almost certainly miss the ceremony. I blush to admit that I yelled and kicked the flat tire.

Then I noticed that the Old Shaman was no longer in the car but squatting in the meager shade of a pinyon tree. And he was *smiling*! When I went over to him, grumbling that we'd probably have to spend the night out here, he said:

"Come sit here in the shade with me, my son. I wonder what adventure we are going to have next."

I sat down beside him as if shot, thunderstruck. Whereas I had been heavily invested in reaching our destination and sticking to the agenda, which attachment was only raising my blood pressure and making me grumpy as all get-out, he was accepting the present reality—*and looking forward with excitement to what would happen next* like a kid at Christmas. While I had been making myself feel terrible by cursing our misfortune, he expected an adventure.

I sat under the little tree with him, taking some slow, calming breaths as he had taught me. Ten minutes later we heard a vehicle approaching. Just as in the song, good Lord, it was a flatbed Ford. The driver was one of the most beautiful women I had ever seen, wearing a cowgirl hat and a turquoise ring on just about every finger.

"Gollygoshdarn," she said. "You boys look like you could use a lift. Hop in and I'll take you on up to Ojo Caliente. I hear tell there's a big ole fiesta there tonight after my friends get themselves hitched."

Suddenly, it seemed to me providential that we had had a flat and no spare right at this place in the middle of a desert.

The shamanic perspective is one of *inverse paranoia*: You start believing that the Universe is out to do you good.

As we work with releasing our expectations and accepting reality as it is, being in the present moment rather than some other time frame, and being open to the varied mysteries of the others around us, we are walking a profoundly spiritual path. Another important part of this spiritual paradigm shift is, I think, from looking to my partner for what I need to examining *myself* within the larger perspective the Old Shaman has sung of. My partner is then no longer the be-all and end-all but one means among many of journeying on this Earthwalk. This shift helps me let go of any unreal expectations that I might put upon my partner, to see her as a part of the Great Mystery, to take 100% responsibility for my own psycho-spiritual growth, and to accept that for right now we each make this magical Earthwalk upon our green planet as separate beings.

It also helps me to retain awareness on two levels simultaneously, or by shuttling back and forth between them:

1. The level of existential aloneness, in which I am a separate entity, and
2. The level of spiritual Oneness, in which I am a part of the Great Mystery and know that my currently embodied form is but a *part* of Reality.

In our loving relationships we can operate on both levels. We can be catapulted out of separateness and for a time experience ecstatic union. We can then accept our separateness and enjoy being an individual again. What I have found works effectively is to avoid clinging to either state and to allow them to flow as easily as our breathing—the inbreath of union, the outbreath of separation. The quite natural cycle that most human beings have established over millennia is the parting and individuation that comes with the morning's tasks, and then the reunion in the evening. Time apart, time together. It is almost as if we have divided our two levels into the time of Light and the time of Darkness. In the Light we experience our separate, solitary self, while in the Dark we experience Oneness and the Great Mystery.

That well-established cycle of parting and reuniting has been diluted in modern culture, though for most people a sense of it remains. This morning I am writing in my study alone and will see my Beloved little during the day while she swims at the gym and then catches fish and gathers plants at the supermarket. This evening I am going to cook that fish with some brown rice and asparagus for her, then begin watching the last season of *Lost* together in the relative darkness, like children hearing a story around the light of the campfire. Who knows what adventures may unfold? Perhaps a polar bear will come out of the jungle.

Sex is a vivid symbol of this shuttling. Two separate beings are drawn to each other and join, physically. Our bodies become one. After an intense union that can bring a brief sense of Cosmic Oneness, we fall apart, separate but still retaining the hum of the blissful union. We bask in the afterglow. Then we enter sleep separately or perhaps get up to put another log on the fire. We cannot, even tantrically, remain forever in Cosmic Oneness. You will recall what it is like when we hold one hand with another for more than a few minutes. To cling to either pole is to stifle the relationship. We learn to let go of control, to grieve what we have lost and then to move on into what is here now. Many of us sometimes feel the need to weep after orgasm. I encourage everyone to give in to that need, to feel the bittersweetness of weeping with joy and sorrow in your Beloved's arms, and then to kiss your partner with gratitude before you get up to tend your garden.

In the same way that you might allow yourself to be "inappropriate" and to sob after sex, you will sometimes feel anger at your partner. That, too, is a part of the Divine Game. Do not judge its appropriateness by building a mental case. Just let yourself feel the anger. Turn away from your partner at a right angle or go into a separate room and shout it all out. Relish the Dark as well as the Light. The Sufis have a marvelous saying: "You can meditate for ten years and get an inch closer to God. Or you can be really angry and be with God instantly." There are many marked paths into the Great Mystery.

It is by allowing our relationship to breathe, in and out, that we keep it alive and growing. We can do so by having faith that the moving apart and the moving together are both parts of the larger Dance.

As we go through the power struggles that trigger our archaic Pain, we enter the Dark and perhaps become worse than we would imagine ourselves to be. Who is this snippish, stubborn, petty, petulant fool? We come face to face with our Shadow side. If we don't flee, physically or into denial, we then have the opportunity to enter the purifying fire and burn off the old Pain. As we do so, we can heal our wounds and become spiritually whole. (Review Chapter 8, "Feeling Through on Your Own," in *Real Relationship*.)

This is the ultimate gift of long-term relationship: By committing ourselves to growing spiritually and psychologically through the challenges that we face together, we become better than we ever imagined we might be. As we do so, we also discover there is more to Reality than we ever dared hope.

As we go through this process, we will, over and again, experience ourselves as part of larger perspectives: Of the history of great lovers when we are full of love. Of our original families when Pain ascends. Of our generational family as we witness ourselves repeating familial patterns. Of the broader society as we deal with sociological issues such as men's and women's changing roles. And of the spiritual when we continually experience the heights and depths of our feelings.

For me, the most important thing to remember on this journey is that my Beloved is my spiritual companion. Out of all others, she is the one I have selected in some mysterious way as my partner in spiritual growth, just as she has so selected me. Sometimes we will be angry with each other. That is okay. Through our anger we will learn and grow. Sometimes we will be in bliss. That is okay. From our bliss we will learn and grow. Whatever comes to us is grist for the spiritual mill. Through our process together we come to know more of the Great Mystery. This is a path with heart.

Practical Spirituality

I'd like to offer you some practical ways through which you might connect with a spiritual dimension in your life. Pick any that you think might work for you right now. Any spiritual path needs to be a "path with heart," that is, one you feel powerfully drawn to:

1. A continuing theme throughout this book—and in *Real Relationship*—has been that as we work with ourselves to become better partners in our relationships we will necessarily become better people. If I'm a hermit it doesn't impact others if I speak in derogatory ways; it certainly matters, however, if I'm in relationship, and, as I learn to speak in a kinder and more compassionate language, I find I am becoming a kinder and more compassionate person.

2. While it is true that I have on occasion grumbled about how traditional religious organizations can be counter-spiritual, they can be a mighty bulwark to our spirituality. I was exceptionally fortunate, as a child, that my parents chose a wonderful Episcopalian minister to shepherd their children in our early spiritual education. Reverend Raymond Davis encouraged his flock to think for themselves rather than swallow dogma, and he showed a social consciousness and moral courage in integrating his church in Virginia after the *Brown v. Topeka* decision of 1954. He was the one who encouraged me to think more deeply about the nature of the universe and its many mysteries. If you are already in a traditional religious organization that promotes true spirituality, great. If you were as a child but no longer practice, you might find it helpful to return to your spiritual roots. Carl Jung pointed out that there is always a potential richness there.

3. Create time to be quietly alone. Our inner spiritual voice is a still, small voice that is easily drowned out

by the constant noise and fidget of our culture. When I first began backpacking in the High Sierra, I noticed that for the first day or two that I was in Nature's silences I could hear a faint humming in my ears. I finally deduced that it was a kind of "white noise" that my brain had put in place to screen out the worst noises of the city I spent most of my time in. I literally had limited hearing. Once that white noise dissipated, I found that a sharper hearing returned and I could hear both what was outside and what was inside with much greater acuity. I suggest that you set aside at least 20 minutes each day to sit or lie down in a quiet place and tune in to your deeper Self. I also suggest that you set aside at least one week each year to be alone in quiet. Yashi likes to do so in a silent meditation retreat, while I prefer being out in Nature. You might enjoy going on a Vision Quest.

4. Spend time with Nature. If you are a city-dweller, this will be more challenging. Grow a houseplant. Keep a pet. Find a park that uplifts your soul. When you have time off, go into the country to hike, backpack, kayak, or just sit on the beach to immerse your mind in the rhythms of the waves. Even if you live, as we do, on quiet, wooded acres, create time each year to venture into the deep wilderness. Our national park system has been called "America's best idea." It probably is. Take advantage of this wonderful legacy to stretch your lungs in the kind of air humans breathed for many eons and your legs in gorgeous country.

5. Practice mindfulness meditation. You can begin immediately by sitting alone in a darkened, quiet room for twenty minutes a day, focusing your attention on your breath. I would suggest that you take a one-day or weekend or three-week workshop to help you go deeper. Blaise Pascal, the great French philosopher, said, "All of man's troubles stem from his inability to sit quietly in a room alone." If, like me, you find sitting hard to do, begin with shorter periods. For instance, I like to begin my day with a moment of gratitude that I am alive to live another day. I go outside and face the rising sun and say "Thank you, Father Sun, for this day and this life." At the end of the day I watch the sunset and review what I did that day that I feel contented about.

6. When we mark the day or season or year with a repeated action, we have created or joined with a *ritual*. The problem with rituals is that they have a tendency to become rigid and demanding rather than helpful and liberating. Give yourself the freedom to participate in and modify those rituals you enjoy while avoiding feeling guilty if you are not a strict observer of them. If I miss a sunset, I don't beat myself up about it. What little rituals help you connect to Spirit? I still love to sing the hymns of my youth and to observe much-modified forms of Hannukahmas and Eastover. And on the Winter Solstice we delight in emulating our Druid forebearers by leaping over an outdoor fire to mark the returning of the Light.

7. Read the great myths of the ages. They illuminate the human psyche, if you can understand that they are metaphorical rather than literal. Heroes didn't slay actual dragons guarding piles of treasure, but the hero in each of us must confront and overcome our own greed in order to enjoy true spiritual treasures. Read Joseph Campbell, who performed a great service for us all in his explications of the mythic and in showing how to apply that age-old wisdom to our current lives.

8. Continue to explore your own unconscious realms to bring back the vast treasures that are secreted there. Write down your dreams and work with them. Share them in the mornings with your partner. When your relationship kicks up a big feeling, give yourself space to process it, seeking its primal roots, rather than dramatizing it in the relationship. Go into such feelings on your own, with your partner holding the space for you, or with a feeling therapist. Switch your attitude from perceiving feelings as inconvenient to seeing them as gateways into a rich world of discovery.

I wish you well in this exciting quest.

CHAPTER 8:

CONCLUSION

Having read this book as well as *Real Relationship*, you will no longer have the illusion that long-term relationships are easy. You know they are a lot of hard, hard work. While it is true that a short-term or sometime relationship can be easy, or at least easier, they are unlikely to provide you with the following benefits of a vivid long-term relating:

1. Of necessity, you will gradually release your False Self and become the person you really are. You will learn to feel deeply and express yourself openly. You will become intimately acquainted with anger, bliss, grief, and fear. You will discover that you can be loved for your True Self. You will become more authentic and honest.

2. You will learn about another person's True Self, what really makes him or her tick behind the *persona* and the need to be "good." You will learn how to accept someone as they really are, rather than as you want them to be. You will learn compassion.

3. You will learn how to speak up for what you want and how to negotiate solutions to a conflict-of-needs situation. If you do not learn these skills, you will become depressed—and learn from the depression, if you don't take pills.

4. You will learn how to elegantly balance intimate togetherness with individual separateness, and you will value both. You will learn how to form appropriate fences to enhance separateness and gates to facilitate intimacy.

5. You will learn how to have adventurous sex within a deep safety.

6. You will develop a kind and compassionate sense of humor. Remember, if you can laugh at your troubles, you'll always have something to laugh at.

7. You will come to accept the ups and downs of life and relating, expecting them rather than wishing life could be constant bliss. You will learn to see the opportunities for growth and learning in both.

8. You will come to see yourself and your relationship not as the be-all and end-all but as a small part of a huge Universe—and you will come to feel a happy connection to the All.

Real relationship is not for sissies. There will be tears and much-pounded pillows as well as blissful love-making and pillow-talk. But once you have co-created such a connection, you will be in awe of its value—and you will realize just how challenging it is to create. You will then *know* that what you have with your partner is more precious than rubies and you will also know that, though a new attraction might seem tempting, building it into a real relationship would take years of hard work. The practical part of yourself will then be inclined to keep the goodness that you have rather than throw it away for a fling that is unlikely to develop into what you now have. As I said before, it's as if you already have a cozy home on a beautiful piece of land with a lake and hundreds of lovely trees, an organic garden and a view of snowcapped peaks—would you toss that away for the possibility of homesteading an unknown bit of ground that might well turn out to be fallow? You know pretty precisely how much work it will take to turn any ground into a garden and how hard it is to construct a rainproof dwelling.

This knowledge will also be a bit scary, for you will come to know how valuable your partner and your relationship are to you—and you will dread the possibility of losing something of such great value. If you do lose all that, through the death of your partner, for instance, you will need to grieve that loss deeply. That, too, will be hard work. If you must go through such a grief, please get help with working through the feelings. You will be able to do so, in time.

Then you will have to decide whether it is worthwhile to begin again to build a real relationship. Younger people usually wish to do so. Having once experienced real relationship, they know its value and know they have the time and energy to co-create another. Older people sometimes decide it isn't worth the effort and may settle for a hermitage or for friends with benefits. In fact, I recently read a study, which I am sorry to say I cannot find to refer you to, which said that half of all single women over 50 were choosing the latter option rather than remarriage. As in all situations, there is no one right way: You would need to search your heart for what is right for you. A good therapist can be invaluable in doing so, as well as working through the grief.

A good therapist can also be very helpful in growing your relationship. Do not hesitate to seek such help for yourselves. We do. It can also be extremely helpful to be in a couples' group. When you see that others are dealing with the same challenges that you are, you will not feel so alone, and you will learn from how they confront their issues.

Early in our relationship, we combined the two by spending an entire week in a residential couples' group held at the Silverado Country Club that focused upon growing relationships—from nine to five daily. That was intense. In the evenings we'd stumble back to our condo (it was owned by Joe DiMaggio, which I, as a baseball fan, got a kick out of— Marilyn slept in this same bed!) to watch old shows from *Star Trek* on TV so we could numb out for a while. Inhalation, exhalation. Many churches and synagogues offer free couples' groups that meet on a weekly basis. Any relationship will benefit hugely from a support system. The very fact that you are checking into your relationship at predictable times with others who are also mindful is extremely helpful.

In this book we have made quite a journey together. It is my hope that you will have found something of value herein for you and your relationships. If you have questions or comments, do not hesitate to contact me at beldenjohnson@att.net. I am happy to hear from my readers, though please understand that I do not have time to respond to all of you. If you wish to go deeper into any of the suggestions I have made in this tome, please consult the bibliography that follows, in which I list a few of the books that I have found particularly valuable.

May this path with heart rise up to meet your feet and may you walk in great beauty all your days.

SELECTED BIBLIOGRAPHY

Barbach, L., *For Yourself: The Fulfillment of Female Sexuality* (1976).
_____, *For Each Other: Sharing Sexual Intimacy* (1984).

Baumeister, R. and Tierney, J., *Willpower* (2011).

Begg, D., *Rebirthing: Freedom from Your Past* (1999).

Bergner, D., *What Do Women Want? Adventures in the Science of Female Desire* (2013).

Brizendine, M.T., *The Female Brain* (2006).

Campbell, J., *The Inner Reaches of Outer Space: Metaphor as Myth and as Religion* (1986).

Castaneda, C., *The Teachings of Don Juan: A Yaqui Way of Knowledge* (1968).

Chamberlain, D. B., *Babies Remember Birth* (1989).
_____, *The Mind of Your Newborn Baby* (1998).
_____, *Windows of the Womb: Revealing the Conscious Baby from Conception to Birth* (2013).

Cousins, N., *Anatomy of an Illness* (1979).

Covey, S., Merrill, A., & Merrill, R., *First Things First* (1994).

Covington-Carter, D., and Carter, L., *Falling in Love Backwards: An unlikely tale of Happily Ever After* (2013).

DeSteno, D. and Valdesolo, P., *Out of Character: Surprising Truths About the Liar, Cheat, Sinner (and Saint) Lurking in All of Us* (2011).

Easton, D. and Hardy, J., *The Ethical Slut: A Practical Guide to Polyamory, Open Relationships & Other Adventures* (2009).

Farrell, W., *The Myth of Male Power* (1993).

Fisher, H., *Why We Love: The Nature and Chemistry of Romantic Love* (2004).
_____ *Why Him? Why Her? Finding Real Love by Understanding Your Personality Type* (2009).

Friday, N., *My Secret Garden: Women's Sexual Fantasies* (1974).

Glass, L., *The Complete Idiot's Guide to Understanding Men and Women* (2000).

Golas, T., *The Lazy Man's Guide to Enlightenment* (1972).

Guerney, B., *Relationship Enhancement* (1977).

Harley, W.E., *His Needs, Her Needs: Building an Affair-Proof Marriage* (2008).

Janov, A, *Imprints: The Lifelong Effects of the Birth Experience* (1983).

Joannides, P. & Gross, D., *The Guide to Getting It On* (1998).

Johnson, B., *Real Relationship: Essential Tools to Help You Go the Distance* (2011).

Johnson, N., *All Natural: A Skeptic's Quest to Discover if the Natural Approach to Diet, Childbirth, Healing, and the Environment Really Keeps Us Healthier and Happier* (2013).

Keleman, S., *The Human Ground: Sexuality, Self & Survival* (1975).

Leboyer, F., *Birth Without Violence* (2009).

Lowen, A., *Love and Orgasm: A Revolutionary View of the Role of Love in Sex* (1965).

Moody, R.A., *Life After Life* (1975).

Maslow, R., *Motivation and Personality* (1954).

Masters & Johnson, *Human Sexual Response* (1966).
_____, *The Pleasure Bond* (1970).

Masters, Johnson, & Kolodny, *Sex and Human Loving* (1982).

Noble, E., *Primal Connections: How our experiences from conception to birth influence our emotions, behavior, and heath* (1993).

Offet, A., *The Sexual Self* (1977).

Perel, E., *Mating in Captivity: Unlocking Erotic Intelligence* (2007).

Pinkson, T., *The Flowers of Wiricuta: A Journey to Shamanic Power with the Huichol Indians of Mexico* (1997).

Reich, W., *The Function of the Orgasm* (1942).

Rozak, T., *The Voice of the Earth* (1992).

Sanford, J., *The Invisible Partners: How the Male and Female in Each of Us Affects Our Relationships* (1980).

Segal, D., *mindsight: The New Science of Personal Transformation* (2010).

Solomon, M. and Tatkin, S., *Love and War in Intimate Relationships* (2011).

Staheli, L., *"Affair-Proof" Your Marriage: Understanding, Preventing and Surviving an Affair* (1997).

Staheli, L. with Weiss, S., *The Complete Idiot's Guide to Affair-Proof Love* (1999).

Street, R., *Modern Sex Techniques* (1959).

Tatkin, S., *Wired for Love: How Understanding Your Partner's Brain and Attachment Style Can Help You Defuse Conflict and Build a Secure Relationship* (2011).

Tolle, E., *The Power of Now* (1999).

Schnarch, D., *Passionate Marriage: Keeping Love & Intimacy Alive in Committed Relationships* (1997).

Weiner-Davis, M., *Divorce Busting* (1992).

Weinstein, M., and Goodman, J., *Playfair* (1980)

Welwood, J., *Journey of the Heart: Intimate Relationships and the Path of Love* (1990).

Zukov, G., *The Seat of the Soul* (1989).

APPENDIX A:
THE TIME MANAGEMENT GRID

	Sunday	Monday	Tuesday	Wednesday	Thursday	Friday	Saturday
6 a.m.							
7 a.m.							
8 a.m.							
9 a.m.							
10 a.m.							
11 a.m.							
12 p.m.							
1 p.m.							
2 p.m.							
3 p.m.							
4 p.m.							
5 p.m.							
6 p.m.							
7 p.m.							
8 p.m.							
9 p.m.							
10 p.m.							
11 p.m.							
12 a.m.							

ABOUT THE AUTHOR

As I was writing this book, I felt extremely fortunate to have four grandchildren—Josie, Torin, Keelan, and Jules—born to very loving parents. Holding each of them for the first time has been an experience I cannot put into words. As I begin witnessing them growing up I feel unbounded joy.

I cannot pretend that the world they will have to navigate is the one I would have wished and did my best to create for them. I can still remember how I felt during the sixties when it seemed possible, even likely, that we would make a better world—and I think we did, for a little while.

I dedicated myself to becoming the change I wished to see in the world—and to assisting other changelings upon the path, especially in their relationships. And so I dedicate this book to my grandchildren and to all the children of the forthcoming world in the hopes that despite the forces of greed and wars and changing climate they will at least start from a wiser place in their intimate relationships. Those positive relationships may yet change the world into the better place we dreamed of creating.

Meanwhile, I continue to work on myself and my own relationships, to write as truly and well as I can, and to have a lot of fun. Presently I am playing on two slow-pitch softball teams, swimming in the Yuba River, and gearing up for two weeks of backpacking in the High Sierra next month.

I much relish sitting on the west-facing deck we built to watch the sunset with Yashi, to whistle in the bluebird family for their feast of worms, and to listen to the wild ululations of the local coyotes in the night. As I grow older, I notice that I find bliss in simple things.

I wish to have the time and energy to write the novel I began 50 years ago, based upon the astounding true story of my namesake, Belden Knapp, who was a hero of the Civil War. An idealistic Union boy from the Finger Lakes of New York, he fell in love with a Rebel gal, was imprisoned in and organized the only escape from Libby Prison, and walked home through enemy territory with two musket balls in his chest. Along the way he decided it was "a rich man's war and a poor man's fight." Keep an eye out.